This book is about determination, willpower, and staying focused while following that dream in life, combined with happiness, love, fun, and friendship... and a few pitstops in between.

Sesky inspired me to do this, as just a normal everyday person exploring life and chasing goals. For me, putting pen to paper was following another of my many dreams, but I would never have done it without sharing my life with her.

I DEDICATE THIS BOOK TO

My amazing horse, Sesky, and all our wonderful times together. From the moment I first got her in 1990, when she was four years old, we enjoyed 28 years of riding, fun, adventure, love, and an everlasting bond.

D1610313

About the Author

B eing young, positive, and competitive from an early age, I always knew that I had determination and liked to chase my goals. Being a competitive runner for years at Scottish Schools level set me on the path to staying focussed on what I wanted.

I worked hard in office jobs straight from leaving school, but nothing could have prepared me for the sudden change in career path that followed just over ten years later. And even bringing up three children never stood in the way of working, as I successfully juggled family life and a new career.

I first became involved with horses and ponies in 1988 purely by chance, when my daughter started riding and later got a pony. I had no knowledge of horses and ponies to begin with, but I learned to ride and soon became the owner of my own horse. As I had always dreamt of owning a horse, I was over the moon, and happily adapted to stable work and outdoor life on top of work and family commitments. But my whole outlook changed completely when I got Seskinore, my second horse, in 1990.

Sesky, as she was known, brought out that determined competitive spirit in me once again, and I began to look at life from a different angle. What had started as a hobby became my passion, and I developed a growing desire to learn and to share my experiences with others through teaching. With hard work and sheer willpower, I became a Qualified TRSS Centre Operator, then gained my Diploma in Equestrian Tourism. Then I carried on working through the grades to become a BHSS Accredited Professional Coach, throwing in the other SVQ Assessor qualification and other bits and pieces needed to fulfil these roles.

In 1994, I opened up my Approved Riding School and Trekking Centre, which gained four-star approval from the Scottish Tourist Board, and which I ran for 20 exciting and enjoyable years. This success shows that age does not prevent you carrying out whatever you desire to do.

Despite experiencing certain changes and challenges in life, staying focussed on what was best and being able to adapt has helped me along the way. And with one particularly dramatic change in life in 2014, I was able to stay strong and carry on, setting a new path in life once again, and eventually taking on a new career.

I have proved to myself that life is there for everyone to live and enjoy; it is never too late. This everyday girl with an everyday horse and a bucketload of great memories did just that – and you could, too.

For more information visit:

www.dynamicdreambooks.co.uk

Introduction

B efore you start to explore this adventure, let me introduce myself and Sesky to you.

Willpower, even from an early age.

My name is Janette McKeague.

Being born into the middle of a large family, with four brothers, three sisters, and limited wealth, I learned from an early age that whatever you have is everything, and that life is what makes you happy.

I only needed my feet, determination, and health, then everything else could just fall into place.

I took to sport in primary school as a runner, and followed that dream for several years. Throughout that time, I always set my goals to reach that finish line, and my determination ensured that I always did.

As time went on, though, I became less content with running short distances. Always keen to push myself further, I started to compete at longer distances, adding in some bumpy cross-country courses along the way as part of my tough training regime, and various competitions.

Running was everything to me. I'd even dodge the odd classes at school just to throw in some extra training time. After school, I'd pound the streets and fields for hours – even running home from my friend's house at night, rather than taking the bus. The run home assisted with some additional training, and saved some extra pennies. And I'm sure the thought of my dad standing at the top of the stairs if I was late was what made me run faster!

All my efforts paid off when I was included in the young Scottish Schools running team some years later, and had the opportunity to travel around the country to compete. The furthest we travelled at that time was to a meeting in Wales, which seemed like the other side of the world for me, as my family never had holidays.

After a year or two of competing, my mum and dad bought me my first pair of running spike shoes for a track competition. I could not believe it – to me, these were like gold!

However, as I wasn't used to wearing running spikes, on the day of the competition I got stuck on the starting line! My spikes were pushed so hard into the ground that I gave myself a bad start, and had to run doubly fast to get placed. Where were my good old trainers when I needed them?

Mum, Dad, and the family had all come to watch me at the competition – something they did not usually do – so I didn't have the heart to tell them about the problem with the spikes.

As a youngster, I had always dreamt about owning a horse or pony, but never thought it would ever happen in real life. Then as I got older, life changed, and buying a pony for my daughter led to me owning my first horse, followed by a second. And that was really the beginning of an amazing partnership.

As I had absolutely no experience at the time with horses and ponies, I had to learn pretty quickly about what to do. Thankfully, I met Iona Drummond, who was on the yard where I used to keep my daughter's pony, and who is still my best friend and soulmate!

Iona taught me how to look after the pony and horse, and how to ride. She was a qualified instructor and a nurse, which came in handy with the number of times I fell off. It was certainly a right pain in the bum at times! Throughout the following years, Iona inspired me to expand my knowledge and eventually to sit exams to become qualified to teach, like her.

She even gave me copies of her notes, which were a great help, as this meant I could home-school myself while bringing up a young family of three and working from home. With her encouragement, I decided I was not too old to follow my passion for horses, and to share my knowledge and teaching with other people.

Alongside my home studies, I began attending training days to sit my TRSS (Trekking and Riding Society of Scotland) exams. This included some stays at training centres, and through time I qualified as a Centre Operator. I followed this by gaining my Diploma in Equestrian Tourism, and operating my own Approved Centre for 20 amazing and successful years.

During this time, I met some fabulous people in TRSS, including Susan, who was always there at the other end of the telephone if anyone needed any help or advice, and George Tait, who had a great deal of experience, and both examined and taught me a lot. I later became an examiner with the TRSS, and often shared exam days with George and a few others. I remember thinking that I always learned something new every time I listened to George giving one of his talks.

On one particular occasion, in the early days of my training, he was leaning over the stable door on an incredibly early frosty morning in the north of Scotland, and said something that has stayed with me over the years. 'Janette,' he told me, 'I have a great saying: "Be as early as you like, but NEVER be LATE!"' Then he just smiled and walked away.

That particular morning, I had been one of the first out – at about 5.30am – and had noticed George looking at his watch when he walked past. By that time, I had already been up the hill to collect my horse from the muddy field, and had started mucking out the stable.

I was always one to be early for anything. Maybe that is why I am always at least half an hour early for my work, even now!

I went on to sit my BHS (British Horse Society) exams and my Riding and Road Safety exam, which were all helpful when I set up my riding school and trekking centre, and for teaching. Over the years, I went on to become a qualified BHS coach, but still carried on with my own training and exams while running and teaching in my centre.

Eventually, when I gained my qualification as a BHS UKCC Level 2 Accredited Professional Coach, I decided I had reached the level where I wanted to be. So, no more exams for me! Along with all my other qualifications, I was also an NVQ Trainer and Assessor, which helped me to pass on my knowledge, experience, and understanding to trainees, and to assist them in achieving their own qualifications.

Throughout the book, you will learn how Sesky and I developed a partnership which changed and developed us both, and proved that age and time do not matter. Whatever your dream, you can work to achieve it.

She taught me NEVER to give up, to carry on, and to believe in what you dream. What you believe, you can achieve!

Sometimes, along the way, you may have to adapt and change to whatever comes your way, as life is just one great big learning curve. But Sesky and I found this out, and learned how to succeed together.

Sesky was my main Trek Leader horse for many a year, and we shared some interesting and eventful trekking experiences! I guess that helped to keep her fit for the work, along with a bit of novice showjumping and the normal riding she did with me on our own. By the time she reached the great age of 32 years young, she was still fit enough for her usual treks around the country roads, along with her work in the school, which she still thrived on.

In Sesky's earlier years, I also bred some lovely foals from her. This was such a beautiful experience, and I have many lovely photographs of those times. Watching Sesky with the foals as they grew up was just amazing.

In time, life and circumstances changed, and I gave up working full-time with horses and teaching. But although I worked in a different job, I carried on with some freelance teaching and still do offer some lessons, though more as a hobby. While I still really enjoy teaching, I have to admit it is now more difficult to fit into my busy life.

A few years ago, with Sesky no longer in my life, I decided I needed to find something to replace all the time I'd spent with her. So, I joined the gym. And that turned out to be an amazing and worthwhile decision. Even when the gyms had to close due to Covid-19 lockdown restrictions while I was writing this book, I still liked to set myself a challenge. So I made sure to fit in my daily gym work at home, and walks of over two hours.

My enjoyment with exercise has proved that you are never too old to start something new; at least, that is what I tell myself, anyway.

When the gym is open, I spend a lot of time there doing different things, including various classes, and swimming. I have even started taking part in a spin bike class, where I like to think I challenge the instructors for a good workout and a laugh.

Most of my days off are spent there, and almost every night after work. My youngest son, Michael, who is a personal trainer and has his own gym, tells me that on some days I do more than him, which always makes me smile.

And going to the gym is certainly a lot cheaper than owning a horse! I remember counting up what I would have spent on the activities I did in a normal monthly workout at the gym, and it came to roughly £294. As my Gold gym membership is only £35 a month, that is the equivalent of a round bale of hay that wouldn't have lasted Sesky a month, so I rest my case.

My book has been put together with happiness, love, and memories of a dream that came true with my amazing horse, Sesky. I hope you find the stories uplifting and interesting, and take away whatever lessons or advice that will help you.

THINKING BACK…

Chapter 1

Flying Changes

I was never involved with horses or ponies at a young age, even though I would love to have been. But when I was 27 years old, the decision was made to buy my four-year-old daughter a pony, as she loved her little rocking horse and kept asking for the real thing.

I had no idea then what that would lead to.

Through working with the pony and learning everything that went along with owning it, I decided I would need to learn how to ride so that I would be able to help my young daughter. She was already having regular lessons in a riding school, so I joined up in another one… and my education began.

Having to teach myself how to look after a pony, so that I could pass that knowledge and information onto my daughter, was hard work. But then I met Iona, who offered to show and teach me what was required. She never knew what she was letting herself in for!

About seven months later, I got my first horse, Minstro, and my time was never the same again. He seemed so big to look after compared to my daughter's little pony!

Minstro was a lovely, experienced 14-year-old 15'hh black and white cob, nice and laid-back, and he was the perfect first horse for me.

Although I'd previously had lessons with an instructor in an indoor riding school, it is a whole different experience having your own horse out in the open school and countryside. And owning your own horse is a lot more work, so I still had a great deal to learn.

That is when Iona started to teach me, with many lessons, lots of advice, and probably her tearing her hair out at times in frustration.

The journey, this whole new experience, really started for me with Minstro, who I had for about a year and a half. During that time, he taught me how to have fun and enjoy riding, and was a safe horse on which to learn about riding on countryside roads, tracks, and across the fields. He also gave me the confidence that I could look after a horse properly, and I learned how to jump round a course of small fences. At most of these, he would hardly break out of trot, but sometimes he would eventually move on into a canter, and I had great fun attending my first novice showjumping competitions.

While Minstro was a great first horse for me, I reached a point where I wanted to progress and gain more experience, and that is when I got Sesky in 1990, while Minstro was sold to a lovely lady to continue his riding with her.

Sesky, though, proved to be a very different horse. She was quite a character from the start, and not as laid-back as Minstro! So, my next phase of learning had begun.

*

The novice pairing, 1990.

This amazing horse, who was actually named Seskinore, was born in 1986 in Ireland. An Irish draught cross thoroughbred, she was a beautiful, darkish dapple-grey colour, four years old when I got her, and a little bit bigger than Minstro at almost 15'3hh.

She was also a little bit cheeky at times... as I soon found out!

Prior to coming to me, Sesky had produced a foal, but she had not long been backed and broken when I got her. Compared to Minstro, she was still a novice and quite green, so we both had a lot of work and learning ahead of us. You could say I was quite green, too. Maybe not a good combination to start together, but a great challenge for me!

I guess I could say I taught her a lot, but in return she taught me a lot about how to produce a 'green' horse, as we would say, and to further develop my riding knowledge and my love for horses.

From that very first day, a great friendship grew between us, and Sesky became a huge part of my everyday life.

As the days, weeks, months, and years passed, we both learned new things, had fun, and grew together in experience and friendship. In saying that, there were hard days, especially the times when I fell off. But even then, I loved every minute I spent with her.

My quiet 'me' time involved riding Sesky nearly every day or night, out on our own or in the school, in sunny weather or rain. It never mattered, because she loved to splash through the puddles or over the wet, muddy fields. Riding across the fields, or round the country roads, looking at all the lovely animals, trees, flowers, and the beautiful scenery, while hearing the water running in the burns nearby, was amazing. Just like Sesky.

It was just her and me enjoying our time together, the silence only broken by the distinctive sound of her horseshoes going clip-clop on the road surface, and miming a rhythmic tune as we cantered across the open fields or tracks. The sound of her sweet neighs when she would see something she liked, or her little friends, was always a special moment.

One day in particular that I remember was a trip to the beach, especially as Sesky went into the lorry on her first attempt! Most times, she would run back off the lorry while she was being put on – even when she was clean, groomed, and plaited in preparation for a show.

That beach day was just lovely. A small group of us went along with a few ponies and horses, and thoroughly enjoyed starting our day off with a ride along the quiet shore. I wasn't sure how Sesky would react near the open water, because although she liked puddles, the sea was quite different from passing the burns and rivers she would normally see. Getting her off the lorry was always the easy part, and I remember she came off in a rush, quite excited, so my first job was to try and settle her down to get mounted. Once she had seen where we were all going, she was fine, and just marched along quite briskly. I remember thinking she felt an awful lot taller that day.

We had a great time with all the other horses and ponies walking – more like prancing – along the sand. Thankfully, we had checked the tide times, so the water was out far enough at that point.

Once all the horses and ponies had got used to their surroundings, we all did our own thing for a while. So, Sesky and I were just quite happily trotting about, joining up with the others, then heading away on our own.

After a few canters up and down, we all decided that we fancied a little gallop along the stretch of beach. As we started off, roughly together, I was thinking that it looked a fair distance, and Sesky was getting more excited as we went. So I just turned her slightly away and eventually got her back to canter, then eventually to a walk! My arms were killing me the whole time, as she had been so strong.

Thankfully, with Sesky being my main trekking horse, she did not mind being turned away from the other horses, as it was something she did when I needed her to during a trek with my clients.

The horses and ponies were put back on the lorry for a rest and feed, while the riders enjoyed some lunch of our own before continuing the beach fun in the afternoon.

By that time, the tide had come in a bit, and some of the others were already in the water which was quite far up the horses' tummies. However, Sesky and I were not as brave, and we spent a fair bit of time playing about near the water's edge. Eventually, with a bit of persuasion, Sesky and I decided we would go in a bit further.

Finally, we were prancing again, this time in and out of the water, splashing quite happily. I did not even bother that my riding boots, half chaps, and jodhpurs were getting rather wet, as Sesky was having so much fun.

As time passed, we got a bit braver, and I remember the water splashing at the top of her legs as we started moving in and out of the sea. We were both still enjoying ourselves... then suddenly I found myself sitting on the sand, with the end of Sesky's reins still in my hand! I jumped up quickly, hoping that no-one else had noticed, but thankfully they were all cantering further along the beach. That gave me time to remount and start trotting along again as though nothing had happened, wiping the wet sand off my jodhpurs as I went.

I could not understand what had happened, until I looked down at the ground and saw there were large jelly-fish on the sand, and I realised that they'd given her a fright. When we went back along the beach to where my landing mark was on the sand, I saw jellyfish there, too, so I guess she must have trotted on one and unbalanced a bit, which resulted in me being unseated. At least I hadn't landed in the water, as there's no way I could have disguised drenched clothing from the others!

Grooming the horses' legs for the next week or two after our trip was easy, as the salt water meant their legs were so shiny and easy to clean. Sesky's were almost silver pearl white.

But it was certainly a lesson for any rider to remember, that if you take your horse or pony to the beach, watch out for the jellyfish!

Chapter 2

Growing up

Over the years, Sesky enjoyed a lot of fun and experiences. I knew from when I first set eyes on her that we were going to be a true partnership, and I just loved her from that minute till the last. There was just that instant bond of friendship that carried on throughout our time together.

It didn't take me long to realise, though, that Sesky was quite a character and liked to try and be in charge. As she'd been running in the herd since young, and then having a foal, she was used to doing her own thing, and she liked to keep the other horses in control!

Our riding days, especially in those early times, could be quite amusing. Having to adapt my riding to suit this new horse was sometimes quite difficult for me. Minstro, my first horse, had been quite calm and totally safe, and sometimes took quite a bit of leg on to get going. But now I was on this horse that would just take off if I nudged her a bit too much by accident.

Many a time I was carted off round that outdoor riding arena, hanging onto her neck, desperately trying to stay on. It was like being on a bucking bronco with a mind of its own. The difference between riding Minstro and Sesky was like going from a light aircraft to a jet plane, and there did not seem to be any brakes! It was at times like that I'd wonder where my friend Iona was when I needed her!

Thinking back, I managed to get into a good habit when this did happen. And when I eventually finished my schooling session with Sesky, and was walking round the arena to cool off, I would make out that it had been part of the plan to try and learn my transition work and see if the brakes were beginning to work. After a lot of sweat and determination, I would somehow get Sesky back to a jogging trot and we would then just walk out of the arena with a nice happy smile. I wouldn't like to think which of us looked the hottest, though.

I guess that is where outdoor arenas are great for helping you to cool off and get you both back to nearly pre-riding condition! Unfortunately, though, it all takes place in full view of everybody and anybody on the yard. Heaven knows what my young daughter must have thought as I was flying around the arena while she was about the yard, having ridden her own pony first.

On quite a few occasions in those early weeks, I would end up on the ground, and getting on Sesky, staying on, and getting off at a time of my own choice, became my challenge each time I rode her! Sesky always had that little look of mischief as I was tacking her up, but I think she just enjoyed our tussles – and if I'm honest, I did, too.

Through lots of schooling sessions, and a combination of different schoolwork and just fun days walking about the school or yard, Sesky eventually settled into her new way of life, and I began to get used to the feel of her. She enjoyed the company of the other horses and ponies in the yard and riding alongside them, especially when we were with my daughter and her pony.

Then the lessons with my friend Iona started. And that's when we found out just how strong-minded Sesky could be. In-between our lessons, I would practise on the work I'd been taught to try and improve before the next lesson – or at least try to. Sometimes it would work, but many other times it would not.

One day in our lesson, as we were trotting around the arena and learning her transition from trot to canter, Sesky decided out of the blue to take off. Then, with a massive buck, she dumped me on the ground and jumped over the fence at the corner and out of the arena! Luckily enough, I was on the good side of the fence at the sandy part of the arena, and not on the other side where there was hard ground. Sesky then ran back to her stable, which was just along from the riding arena in the yard. You can imagine what a fright I got, especially as it was the first time I had ever experienced being bucked off!

There was a bit of running about on the yard, as several people had witnessed this. But by the time I ran round, Sesky was standing quite happily outside her stable door with someone beside her. Iona had come after me to make sure I was ok, then checked Sesky, who was fine.

We made a point of returning to the arena to finish on a good note, and Sesky walked back in and stood as if nothing had happened, while all I could think about was whether she would try it again.

Through time, Sesky started on walks up the dirt tracks leading out of the yard, and into the field across the country road for riding. This was another new experience for both of us, but if I'd thought she was lively before, I had a lot of hanging on to do out there. I chose to get my lesson in the field for the first time, and everything was fine in walk, then she started the snorting noise. Although it was by then more like a jog, that slight transition into trot felt to me like an explosion! My nerves were going, especially as there were a few riders in the field at the other side. But Iona calmly told me, 'You'll be fine. If in doubt, hang on!' And that's what I had to do, while Sesky started prancing about and jogging on the spot. If I remember correctly, our first lesson in there was cut short – thank God.

One of my best memories was when I'd take Sesky back down and into the yard, finishing her off when she was cooled down, then going back up into the field and watching my six-year-old daughter, Mari-Claire, having her lesson with Iona, cantering around without a care in the world! It made me wish I could ride like that. To be that confident would just be amazing, and that became my goal. I reckoned if she could do it, so could I.

Sesky got into the routine of being turned out for a while, brought back in and prepared for riding, waiting in her stable until the pony was ready, then we would walk to the arena with my daughter. All the time I'd be thinking, *Right, tonight we are staying on!*

We had so much fun riding. If it were just the two of us in the arena, the pony would canter past Sesky, and I could feel her wanting to canter, too. This proved to be good experience for her, and she learned to go when she was asked and to keep her distance, etc. It was another new skill for her to learn, but as I found out, not one that worked all the time.

My daughter and I in the arena.

When a lot of the horses and ponies were to ride in the arena, Sesky would get more excited, and I would feel as though that buck was just about to come. Knowing now what it felt like, I would prepare myself to try and stay on.

Getting introduced to the trotting poles and different fillers around the arena was good for Sesky at a young age, as she did not seem to be bothered about them. Neither was I, until the day came when my lesson involved taking her over the poles at a controlled speed. This was a tricky job, as Sesky only seemed to have one speed – and it was certainly not controlled.

Initially, when she went over the pole for the second time, she got faster and faster. So, lots of work had to go into the pole work, and eventually we got it right. We could even do four to six poles in a row, and anywhere round the arena, which I was really pleased about.

As my daughter was already confidently going over jumps, I thought it would be a good idea to have this in my next lesson.

Sesky had been bred through the jumping lines from Copper King/King of Diamonds, so I thought she would have good jumping potential. I had only jumped small fences at small, local shows on my previous horse Minstro, which I'd really enjoyed, but I knew I still had a lot to learn. And I soon found out with Sesky that her jump threw me out of the saddle quite often.

Many a time Iona would be shouting, 'Hold on!' as I jumped, and it took a lot of practice for me and Sesky to get it right. Then we added two jumps together, and you guessed it… I came off and landed on the sand with a thump!

The first time she threw me off, Sesky galloped round the arena, jumped out over the fence, and went back to her stable as before. The arena fence was a decent normal wooden one, and I was relieved she hadn't jumped it with me on her back. As she had done it before, I now knew this was Sesky's trick, but it also proved to me that she could jump!

Eventually, with practice, we managed to get it right over the next few months, and we could jump a few obstacles at a time. The lessons carried on, and Iona would stand guard at the corner of the arena where Sesky liked to jump out. And while I worked to keep her riding past, Iona would chase her if she tried to turn and get out. Not amused, Sesky would often take off in canter round the arena, but by now I was learning how to sit on her better and control her back to trot. The next step was to be able to ride quietly past that corner, going in the correct direction, without Iona there!

Mixing Sesky's work with the school, dirt track walks, and a bit of field work with others, seemed to do wonders for her confidence – and mine. We were getting to know each other a lot better, and I was becoming used to her little antics. But just when I thought everything was going well, our next lesson was going to be in the field where the jumps were. All I could hope for was that there would be no-one else around to watch!

The first lesson jumping in the field was hugely different from being in the closed arena with Sesky. She just seemed to feel so comfortable over the fence, and the grass was amazing to jump on. Sesky really enjoyed it, and so did I – particularly as I never fell off!

The first time we completed a small jumping course, I thought to myself, *I have got this!* And I knew Iona was pleased, too. She was probably relieved that I hadn't fallen off, as then we both would have had to chase Sesky around that field to catch her. My daughter was probably thinking to herself, *At last, Mother!* as she was already a little natural at this.

That good finish to the day led us to thinking that Sesky was ready to experience her first ride out along the country road that weekend, rather than just up the dirt track to the field and back again.

Early the next morning, we were up at the yard. Mari-Claire did her mucking out – part of the arrangement for having her pony – and I did Sesky, while Michael was playing and running around as normal in the yard, chasing whatever he could. After my daughter had her lesson, I took Sesky for a short ride in the arena, then Iona and I headed off on the first ride out.

As we walked up the dirt track and out onto the quiet country road, Sesky being Sesky thought she was going into the field across the road for riding. I attempted to turn her round to close the gate, as I wanted her to learn to stand while I did this, so that I could manage if I was   out on my own without having to get off and back on again. But as I went to close the gate, Sesky had other ideas. She pulled quickly round, pushed past the other horse, and headed to the field across the road!

I guess Iona was left to shut the gate. She shouted, but I was too busy grabbing my rein in my other hand and trying to turn Sesky, who was already trotting fast across the empty field, while Iona's voice was disappearing into the distance as we got faster and faster… Our unexpected canter down the field was not exactly a good start to what was meant to be a nice leisurely hack out. But I think Sesky seemed as surprised as me when I managed to get her back to trot in no time.

Once we had reorganised, we headed up the road a bit for a good while, then it was time to head back. A few attempts at trotting were thrown in at different parts, and a few cars passed by, which was good experience for both Sesky and me. When we approached home, the other horses were running about the fields and we had to walk down the dirt tracks past them, but we managed to get back down to the stable yard, off the slight slope of the path, with all four feet of hers still on the ground. Better still, we managed to close the gate on the way back with no mishaps this time, and I was still in the saddle!

FIRST HACK COMPLETE.

I'm sure Sesky had loads of extra carrots and Polo mints that afternoon, and the question from my children on my return that day was, 'Did you stay on?' Naturally, my answer was 'Yes', without adding in the other bits. Unknown to them, Iona and I were grinning at each other as we walked to the stables; I just had to have a good laugh!

Our riding days and lessons through time were becoming quite varied. We had the benefit of the field on good days for riding in or just a simple walk round, but we also had enjoyable rides out along the country road. Some days, it looked like we were leg yielding from one side of the road to the other, when Sesky would shy away from the other horses or some things, but she never seemed to bother leading to the country trails. The riding arena was always there for that extra bit of work or to walk round, and as we both improved in there, there was no longer any jumping out for Sesky.

The lunge lessons had started for Sesky, and it was nice for me to watch while Iona lunged her at the start, before she showed me how to do them. But when it came to me having the lunge lessons on Sesky, it was a completely different matter! I didn't enjoy that as much, because they were a lot harder, especially later without the stirrups! But I guess they did help to improve my balance a great deal. This is where the riding arena was useful. I had never imagined there would be so much to learn.

After having lessons in the field and jumping, I was becoming more comfortable and confident with Sesky. We had been hacking out up the roads and through the off-road tracks with friends, but my next challenge was to do this on my own.

I thought a good time to do this would be while my daughter was having her lesson. I decided I would ride Sesky up after her and into the field, and work about, knowing Iona was there teaching and on hand if anything did not go to plan. I could have some controlled trots and canters up in the top corner and around the edge of the field. My plan was to finish with some nice, controlled trots around the whole field, and a leisurely walk back down and then to the stable, with me smiling from ear to ear once I had accomplished this. All went well, and the first part of my challenge was achieved. Sesky just seemed to thrive on her work and really enjoyed it each time. She just never seemed to tire.

The second part of my challenge for another day was to ride Sesky on my own up the road and back, in time for my daughter's lesson finishing. That way I could concentrate solely on Sesky and be prepared for anything out of the ordinary.

I remember leaving just after the pony went to the field for its lesson, then I mounted up in the yard and headed up the track through the field to the top of the road. As arranged, the gate was closed over but not locked in, so I only had to get Sesky turned round to close the gate properly this time. I thought that would be better than having to get her to stand while I opened and then closed it. I was aware that the lesson was going on in the field and that other horses were riding in there, too, so I did not want to be standing about too long at the gate trying to open and close it. The quicker I could get Sesky along the road and away from there, the happier I'd be.

We were no sooner walking along the road than the first car passed us. Thankfully, the driver had gone nice and slow and wide, so Sesky hardly even took any notice. Along we went happily on our first hack out alone. The morning was lovely and dry, with a bit of sun, and the birds chirping happily in the trees. A perfect riding day.

Along the quiet country road, we did a few trots and walks, then the trots got a bit longer. Sesky was getting a bit more excited, as it was all new to her being out on her own. One or two other cars passed on our way out and when we turned round to come back, but again Sesky had not been bothered by them.

I took her into one of the small dirt tracks that went off-road, to turn her round, and she turned quite happily then we headed back home. I did not want the first hack out to be too long, as I did not know how Sesky would react, and obviously I did not want to be too far away from home if she started playing up. But happily, it all went amazingly well. With only one or two side steps thrown in here and there, I could not complain, and we reached the yard and the stable just after the lesson had ended.

I think my whole body was smiling that day, and for Sesky there were more Polo mints by the handful , and plenty of carrots. MISSION ACCOMPLISHED YET AGAIN!

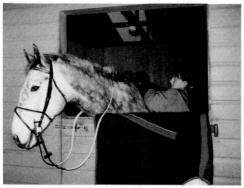

Sesky being untacked after one of our adventures.

The next hack out a week or two later was with a group, but this one proved to be a bit more exciting. When we passed a tractor or two that day, Sesky got a bit jumpy, because one of the other horses did not like them and had reversed into Sesky, which unsettled her. However, she soon calmed down as we carried on up the road. Passing the tractor again on the way down was better, as Sesky was at the back of the ride and not near the jumpy horse. Surprisingly enough, she just walked past it as she raised her head a little, gave a little sideways sway, had a look, then carried on as if it were not there. I gave her a little pat on the neck, saying, 'Good girl, Sesky,' just to let her know I appreciated that. We were both happy.

Being out with the other horses and ponies obviously made the trotting a bit different, as they were all more excited in company, trying to catch up with the ones in front or beside them. But the hacks proved enjoyable and good experience for us all.

Most weekends, when the weather allowed, we would all go out up the country roads, along the dirt tracks past the water, through the trees and fields. As you might imagine, with the different natures of the horses and ponies, things did not always go to plan, but as Sesky and I became more confident, we just went along with whatever and took it in our stride! It was all part of the learning curve.

At least once or twice a week I would make a point of getting Sesky out on her own, so that she would not rely on company for going out. Here we would venture into different roads, dirt tracks, and pathways that we had not been to before. Finding new routes and trails was the highlight of our day, and as we got more experienced at these parts, the odd canters were thrown in along the dirt tracks and the off-road tracks. I loved teaching and showing Sesky new things and places, and I guess she loved it, too. We had so much fun together.

Although Sesky was young and had only been learning over the year, she was beginning to seem like an older horse in a young body, maturing and grasping all her new things and enjoying life. It made our time together so much better when Sesky would now just go quite happily out from the yard on her own, or enjoy her ride   with company, standing without a fuss while I opened and closed gates, and separating happily from other horses as they went to the field and we headed along the road. Most times we'd pass a few cars while being out, but she never bothered about them. I guess that being on the yard with lots of cars coming and going, and the tractor going about, had got her used to the noise and helped her to cope when out on the country roads.

As time went on, having both a horse and pony in livery on a yard was becoming quite expensive. And travelling back and forward for quite a distance from the far side of the city to the other each day, while juggling family life with three young children, was becoming difficult and took quite a lot of organising. So eventually, roughly within a year of getting Sesky, we moved to our own farm.

Chapter 3

New Adventure

The farm was just incredible. Although it had been derelict for a few years and needed a lot of work, I reckoned it had a lot of potential, and there were several outbuildings which would come in particularly useful. Having lots of land was like heaven for the horse and pony.

I remember the first time I took a run out into the countryside near Loch Lomond to see it. I had been up at the livery yard, which was a good distance away, although nearer to the farm than where we lived at the time. However, I did not know that other side of the countryside, and as there was no satnav in cars in those days, it was likely to be an adventure to find the place. I did what I still do now and, with the pen and paper out, drew my directions with scribbles and circles that only I really understood (I'm certainly no artist!), then headed off with one of my friends and the children in the car.

It was a lovely sunny afternoon, and eventually I found myself driving up this big, long, bumpy driveway with fields at either end. In front of you as you reached the top near the courtyard, were outbuildings and barns. Oh, yes, and the farm cottage! I have to admit, the cottage was the last thing on my mind, as my brain was whirling at seeing so many outbuildings and the potential for stables. I was in heaven!

Even though the farm was not ours yet, it just seemed like home from that minute on. While the children were running about, looking in and out of the outbuildings and climbing where they should not have been, I was in dreamland thinking of what this place could be like and how Sesky would just love the fields and all that green grass.

We spent most of the afternoon there, excited at the possibilities. *Could this be our new home?* Thinking back, I did not even look through the windows of the farm cottage– until the last few minutes. It just didn't seem important. I was too busy thinking about Sesky, the pony, the children, and what we could do with all these facilities and wonderful space.

Through time, we were lucky enough to move into this beautiful part of the country, not far from Loch Lomond. The view of the loch from the farm was just stunning in all weathers, and it was a place where Sesky and I would find lots of trails and rides to go on.

I must admit that initially I was a bit wary of moving out into the countryside. Being used to living in housing estates with lots of streetlights, I had always thought of the country as being dark. But once when I mentioned this to my dad, he told me, 'The countryside is as light as you want it to be, and is not dark.' I always kept that in mind, and through time I got to see what he meant. He loved the countryside, so I thought he should know best.

The first day moving into the farm was so exciting. That night, we decided to leave Sesky and the pony out in the field. They had done this in the other yard at times, but this time they were going to be in a field of their own. However, I hadn't thought about leaving them with all that lush grass. So the next morning, I was lucky that they were all right, as too much grass can be harmful to them if they gorge on it.

I had been up at the crack of dawn to bring them into their temporary stables which we'd made the previous day from the cattle pens that were already there. We'd cleaned and washed out the cattle pens, and had bedded them down with lovely fresh straw. When we eventually caught them from the field, they were both exhausted from their night of munching and freely running around.

I remember my daughter and I just looking at them and thinking how perfect it was to see them in their own stables, in view of the windows of our new house. We would only have to roll out of bed in the morning to feed them, without even stepping foot in the car. *What more could we want?* It was such a pleasure to have this wonderful opportunity right on the doorstep!

Sesky enjoying her morning rest.

Having them at home made life much easier, and we soon realised how much extra time we had by not having to travel over an hour to see them at a yard. Getting a new routine going soon started to work, although a few times along the way it did get slightly adjusted. I had never seen the children do their homework straight from school so quickly, as the agreement was that once it was done, they could go out and ride, and play, and discover new adventures around the farm.

In the mornings, on opening the window from the house or coming out of the door, it was lovely to be greeted by a neigh from Sesky. Her stable was right opposite the house, with the stable wooden shutters left open for her to look out and see. As time went on, though, it meant there was no chance of sneaking out to do anything else first. The routine was firmly to feed the horse and pony first thing, then get the children fed and off to school.

The family grew a little more when we bought another pony, to give my oldest son, Gerrard, the opportunity to try riding. Tuppins was a lovely Skewbald gelding, maybe about 13'2 in height, and much older and laid back, and very experienced. He was simply perfect to plod about on, a great friend for Sesky and the pony, and he took up that extra stable space that needed filling anyway! Through time, however, Gerrard decided that riding was not for him, and he had no real interest in horses or ponies. Tuppins stayed, of course, and came in handy.

The children all got to pick something for their new home. My daughter had her new pony, Cally, who we bought not long before moving into the farm, so she was happy.

And although the boys tried it out, they found Cally a bit too much to ride and not as quiet as Tuppins. Through time, with boys being boys, they decided they wanted a bit more 'horsepower' and reckoned that a quad bike would be great for the farm – and some extra fun – quickly followed by a dirt bike. I suppose this got Sesky used to the noise as they sped about in the nearby fields, and made her more aware of things to see when out and about the country roads.

Housework did not come high on my agenda now, although it eventually got done. I was more often thinking about the huge project outside, and imagining what could be out there.

Work on the yard soon got started, ripping apart and changing outbuildings and barns that had previously been used for cattle. The huge amount of land also came in handy over all the years by providing the grazing that was needed for the horses and ponies (and yes, as you have guessed, a good few more horses and ponies did follow!).

After the stables were sorted, the next job was to convert the outdoor sileage pit into an outdoor arena. What else would you have expected! This proved its weight in gold over the years, and although it was a bit small, it was wonderful to have an arena to ride in as an option to going out in the fields.

Even though it was not full size, Sesky was able to canter quite happily about there, and she did not seem to mind the walls that were all around it from the old sileage pit. A fence and gate across the front of it made it lovely and safe to ride in, and a good surface meant it was ideal for even doing some jumps. This became our practice place for increasing our height and jumping technique.

Sesky just loved the new routine that we had got into, and we soon fitted in a plan of exercising. With her being young, I wanted her to have plenty of mixed things to do and enjoy, but also to benefit from. We had plenty of school work mixed in with field work, and lots of routes to explore without even venturing out onto the country roads.

The faraway field was extremely useful, as we discovered this had a gate out onto the quiet back country road leading from our own land. Once we had dug the gate out from the overgrown ground around it, we could use this if we did want to explore the countryside routes, which Sesky and I most certainly did.

The driveway leading up to the farm was a good long walk to the bottom, but it led onto the busy main road, and I wasn't ready to cross that yet with Sesky. However, I did take her down a few times just to stand near the bottom of the drive to watch and listen to the fast traffic going passed, trying to get her used to it for the day when we would try it out. We did have a few jumpy moments, especially when the big lorries would zoom past, but it was all good experience for her.

Through time, with the noisy tractors and diggers working about the yard, and different farm traffic and cars, Sesky was soon afraid of nothing. She would quite happily walk past the digger as it worked, and did not even bat an eyelid. I would even take her up to where they were working and just let her stand about and munch the grass while the workers went about their jobs. After all, this was going to be her living environment now, so she needed to get used to these daily happenings.

The fields had plenty of room in them and a lot of different variations of ground, which was a great opportunity for her to learn. In the middle of one of the fields, there was a small, wooded area with not too many trees and bushes, and a burn running through. It was slightly higher on the ground at one side, and a small old wooden fishing boat lay upside down beside it, so this became our fun training area – to jump over the small burn, up onto the bank, and over the boat!

At first, Sesky was not too keen to learn this new skill, and it took quite a few attempts before she would finally follow on behind my daughter and her pony. Within no time, though, Sesky was jumping over the obstacle – sometimes to the side, over a smaller part of the water, but at least we did safely reach the other side. I can remember thinking that she jumped really high over that old fishing boat, but I guess things like that taught her that nothing was scary. When my daughter was not about, the boys would run in front of Sesky and she would follow on, with a good bit of encouragement and nudges from me, and a carrot awaiting her at the other side.

With this area proving to be so much fun, lots of new ideas came into my head, and I thought about getting some ditches dug out to include in this part of the field. Within a month or two, we had about three. One of the small ditches was not too wide, and was just open in the middle; one had some gravel stones filling it; and the other one was slightly wider and situated at a slight angle. Getting over these obstacles proved a lot trickier than jumping over the burn and boat – even for the pony. But with sheer will and determination, after a few days Sesky made her huge flight in the air and attempted her first ditch. The other two ditches had to wait a little bit longer. I think that was probably my decision, though, as I didn't want to fall off.

As time went on, we mastered all three ditches. Adding them in with her usual part of the bank and burn with the boat, we would then carry on to the first ditch, and the second and third just seemed to flow like clockwork. We now had our own little pretend cross-country circuit over a small part of the field, and it became an area that others also enjoyed through time. It was great having the space to play about in whenever we wanted to, and I remember thinking one day, while riding in there: *Is this a dream, or am I really living this?*

The hay field, as we called it, was great in the summer once the hay was cut, as we used the bales to ride around for exercising. The introduction of increasing and decreasing circle sizes came in useful, with a couple of the bales being used as markers. This made things a bit more fun once Sesky got used to seeing them – although I wouldn't stop and stand for a while too close to one in case she would try to eat it. Then we would all have the job of riding around the field and counting them, to see how many were made.

It was really amazing what you could do with a bit of imagination and space. There was a good hill in this field to work up and down, and plenty of field gates to open and close, riding from field to field. I must admit, I did not like the gates which you would have to dismount to open and close, as Sesky wasn't one for standing still while I tried to remount. It was just another new thing for her to learn, but sometimes she would take off into the field before I could get back on, then stand munching the grass, and just watch me marching towards her until I could eventually get back on. Through time these gates were replaced for ones with top opening handles, which made them much easier to use while mounted, and proved extremely useful. Happy, easier days for me, with no more sneaky munching for Sesky!

Walking or riding through the different fields which belonged to the farm was exciting, and we were to find a lot of different things we had yet not experienced before. I will not forget the day when a deer leapt over the fence just ahead of us, causing Sesky to almost jump out of her skin, and me to grab onto her neck to secure myself back down onto my saddle and manage to stay on. This was something we had not seen at our previous yard, because it was much busier and less peaceful, so I hadn't given it any thought. But as time went on, it became second nature to Sesky to see the deer in the fields, either when we were out riding or just when she was grazing next to the others. It was a lovely sight to watch the deer, especially when they had young with them, bouncing along the fields in flight when anyone else was nearby. It always felt like something out of a movie.

The one thing I did not take to in all my years at the farm or being in the countryside – and neither did Sesky – was the pheasants! Those birds made the loudest screeching noise I have ever heard, and would fly out of nowhere, giving us both such a fright. A nice, relaxed walk would then suddenly become a scrambled jumping trot or gallop off!

The time of the pheasant shoots in the countryside in the winter were the worst. Over the years, we eventually got used to this and the gallop off would not happen, but we still got a fright when the birds suddenly took flight. Then, just when we thought the shoots were finished and we would not see the pheasants for another year, out popped the few that had survived the shoot, taking off with a loud screech into the air. As a result, we made sure to be prepared at that time of the year for the sudden appearance of these birds.

Despite my annoyance at them, the pheasants were beautiful to see. The colour in the male bird was lovely, with the mix of chestnut golden-brown colours and black, and their gorgeous red and green heads making them easy to spot. The females, who were brown with a few spots, were harder to notice when they were just walking about in the field or sitting on the fence posts waiting to fly off. Nice to look at, but not to hear!

Our lessons continued with Iona, and Sesky began comfortably and happily jumping around small exercises we had built in the arena, with a few jumps we'd made. Through the week at home, I would have the children put up the jump and move the pole up a hole or two at a time to raise the height, then I would jump over it a few times in preparation for Iona doing the same thing at our next lesson. I always liked to try and be one step ahead and prepared! There was no better feeling than hearing the children shouting encouragingly, 'Come on, Mum, you can do it!' And I did.

Those first exhilarating summer months at the farm just flew in, but one day I was not prepared for was when Iona decided I was to jump through a grid in the field; this is where there are several jumps in a row, one after another. Looking at it at first, I thought that it would be easy, because the poles were all on the ground. Little did I realise that was NOT the way they were going to stay!

After popping over these quite well a few times, the poles then started going up, one after the other. Sesky just took it all in her stride and popped over everything. But before I knew it, these had become actual jumps, and we were getting over them one after the other. When all the poles were finally up, the grid was complete. Sesky really seemed to enjoy it, though, and so did I… until the stirrups were taken away!

I remember wondering how on earth I was expected to jump over the grid with no stirrups, but after a lot of explaining and encouragement – and watching my young daughter and her pony have a shot at it first, before it was adjusted for us – I just had to get on with it. And I'd never been one to refuse a challenge!

I don't think Sesky had much mane left that day (only kidding!), with me grabbing onto it for balance, and trying not to grip my legs up. We made a few attempts at getting over it, and yes, I did fall off, but I was determined not to be defeated. Refusing the offer to have my stirrups back, off through the grid we went again, and with pure will-power and determination we jumped out the other side, still on board – although a bit wobbly. One more attempt and all was well. *Heaven help me*, I thought, *when we would need to jump a decent height.*

Finishing on that good note was always important, so I ignored Iona's suggestion of 'a canter without the stirrups'. A nice walk around the field with the stirrups back was more like it to end what had been another good lesson.

Having the different fields to ride in really helped Sesky to adjust to different terrain, where her balance and stride would need to be altered, and for me to adjust my seat and not fall off.

The nice flat fields allowed Sesky to canter around and open into her first gallop with me. A small decline in part of the field helped me to move her up a gear, and what an experience that was! I remember hoping we had brakes to slow down! But all was well when, finally, her legs seemed to come back into her body and her neck began to shorten, then I could sit back down into the saddle. The experience fairly blew the cobwebs off, and I was thrilled at successfully experiencing my first true gallop. Of course, my little daughter and her pony were ahead of us, galloping round, and Sesky seemed like a giraffe as she trotted around the field before I finally got her to a walk. I think we were both ready to be tucked up for a sleep that night, after such an enjoyable riding day, but I guess all our early schooling days from the start had paid off.

Having the fields is great, but sometimes the horse's shoes come off when riding in there, if they get stuck in the ground. That always leads to that dreaded moment when we check them on coming out, wondering if there will be a panic...

One night that summer, we decided to go for a late ride after dinner. A few of us were playing about in the field, doing different things, and I remember Sesky cantering around about twenty times, without stopping, in such a beautiful, controlled pace. It was just one of those perfect summer evenings, and we stayed there until we realised it was almost 11pm, but it was so good and still so light that I could have stayed all night. That is when I remembered that saying of my dad's: 'The countryside is not dark; it's only as dark as you want it to be.' And I knew exactly what he must have meant.

Luckily enough, we had no lost shoes that night, but as it is something which does happen unexpectedly, you really need a good, dependable farrier. This is when I met Jim and Alison. Jim became our farrier, and he looked after Sesky for many a year, along with the few ponies. Being available to take them on, and being close by, was ideal. Alison was always at the end of the phone for bookings, and to deal with that panic call when Sesky lost a shoe and I needed it desperately back on for riding or for a show. Then Jim was soon there to sort it all out. Panic over.

Chapter 4

Horsepower

Sesky and I had started going to a few unaffiliated showjumping competitions, as Mari-Claire had been taking part for a few years. It wasn't long before Sesky and I got the bug for this, and it was lovely for us to go together, with the horse and pony. It worked particularly well that the ponies jumped first, then the horses.

The shows were a good experience and enjoyable, but I can't say the same thing about towing the trailer – that was a bit of a nightmare! Apart from a quick little lesson in the farmyard, I'd never done it before. And while driving straight was fine, I was apprehensive about trying to reverse. My solution to this was to just leave early! So, off early to the shows we went, then we'd drive in and circle round to park so that I was facing out in the direction for leaving, making sure that no-one could park in front of me, meaning that I would not need to try and reverse. It worked out well when this happened, but there was quite often that one driver that just had to squeeze into the most awkward place and block me in.

Reversing was never my strong point, but it was even harder to figure out how to get that trailer reversed in the correct direction. It took several attempts – and probably several correction words, too. At times, I'd think the Jeep had faulty steering when I looked at my trailer as I was trying to reverse! You will know what I mean if you have ever found yourself in that situation. The other worry was if I had to drive onto grass at a show, rather than concrete roads, as I would often find myself stuck in a rut!

If I remember correctly, Sesky only had a few journeys in the trailer, because she was not amused at going on or coming off. As a result, our day at the show was always extended when she went, and sometimes we would be the last to leave because she was not loading. The only benefit of that, I suppose, was that everyone else had left and so I didn't need to reverse that trailer.

Looking at the rosettes won by Sesky and the pony made all the day's efforts worthwhile, and we could always count on Sesky jumping clear around her little courses, as it was something she began to love to do.

Time passed quickly with so much being done on the farm and attending shows, and eventually my next obstacle to tackle was a horsebox.

Learning how to drive this three-horse lorry soon filled my time. I'd practise day and night, driving about the farm first, and of course reversing, before I ventured out to drive up and down the road a few miles to the roundabout and back. Getting in and out of my driveway was a job on its own, and I had to really concentrate at coming back in, as the angle seemed a bit tight to gauge. But once I found the way to do it, I never looked back. I even found reversing it easier, compared to the trailer – maybe not perfect, but it worked.

I'd thought that having the lorry would be much easier to get Sesky on, but unfortunately it never seemed to go to plan. Most of the time she would be halfway up the ramp, then decide it was not for her, then she would jump off the side and drag me with her. On occasions, she'd break loose and take off up the drive to the top end of the farm. Even parking the lorry against the wall, so that she could not jump off, did not help; she'd somehow manage to reverse quickly down the ramp and off, then away she would go again.

If we were still lucky enough to be holding onto her, and got her quickly turned around then chased her up the ramp, she would eventually go onto the lorry. Then, while we were breathing hard and feeling hot and bothered, Sesky would just stand there munching her hay as if nothing had happened.

The morning or day of shows still required that extra early start if Sesky was going, to get her safely onto the lorry. She did get better at the shows and when we were leaving the competitions later in the day. It was only the first few times that she was difficult, and we'd have to get the pony off and Sesky back on, because the jumping classes were in different orders.

Of course, as always with Sesky, there was the odd time when she would catch us out. Everything had been going perfectly for months on end, then out of the blue, at the last moment, she just would not go on the lorry. On those days, folk from other lorries would try to help, without success. In the end, they'd leave us to try on our own and, after a while, on she would walk. I think those were the times when I just had to count to ten, close the ramp up, and drive away. I could never work out a reason for her being difficult or awkward; it was just Sesky being Sesky.

By going to a lot of different unaffiliated showjumping competitions, my confidence with Sesky was growing, and our next adventure would be to try some cross-country. Initially, it was just a thought, as we'd been playing about in the fields for over a year or so, and enjoying the jumping. But the thought of being in a larger open area which was unfamiliar to me, with all these unusual and solid jumps, put me off.

And even though I'd been around a few small cross-country courses and watched my daughter do them, I was still not tempted to compete at them myself. This was when Iona just happened to say she would ride Sesky round a cross-country course for me, to see how she got on. You could say I jumped at the chance!

Iona decided, to my surprise, that we would go to the next competition on the calendar, which was the Gleniffer Braes cross-country. I was so excited for Sesky, and even more thrilled because I was not the one having to ride it first with her. The days then started to be counted down on the calendar by me. The day before the competition, we walked the course, which was a long one, with what seemed like a huge number of jumps. I could not imagine Sesky, being so young at only six years old, attempting it – never mind even finishing it!

Iona was used to riding these bigger courses with her own horses, so it was a great opportunity for Sesky, and her determination and riding experience would teach my horse, too.

She had ridden Sesky a few times before the day, and over the small jumps at home, but I was still a little worried about what my little horse would do. The day of the competition was drizzly and misty, but we were up and out early to head off to the show. This was one of the mornings when Sesky ran onto the lorry without any bother, but only because Iona had picked us up in her lorry, and before Sesky knew it, she was up and on with Iona's horse.

Sesky was going to be competing in the Novice Class, although it didn't look very novice to me. And once she was tacked up, booted up, tail up, I was just relieved that Iona was riding her and not me!

I can remember it as though it was yesterday! Having watched her at the start line and over the first few fences and tyre jump, I think I must have raced to every point where I could get a glimpse of them, with me and the children shouting, 'GOOD GIRL, SESKY!' every time. I think I must have run miles that day trying to watch them; it was like being back in my cross-country running days as a teenager! When I no longer had them in my view, I waited, hoping to see them come over the finish line and still together.

Did they finish the course? Of course, they did!

It turned out that Sesky had only had one or two refusals, but she'd jumped whatever came in front of her, and finished the course. I was so pleased with her – and obviously with Iona, too. What a friend she was. While Iona headed off to prepare her own horse for a more difficult course, I took Sesky away for a long walk to cool off, be cleaned, and settled down.

That was the beginning of Sesky's cross-country competitions. It was also the first time I had seen Sesky look tired after riding, but she soon had that bounce back in her stride as we walked around the show to cool down.

Being thrilled with Sesky, we did go onto take part in a few cross-country courses before competing in the Gleniffer Braes course again the following year.

At one of the local events we attended, the course included a burn jump, which was much bigger than the one in our field or anything I had attempted with Sesky previously. Knowing what she had jumped before with Iona, I thought that it should not be a problem to her – although I was not so sure about me! My aim was to simply get round the course and cross that finish line... together.

About halfway round, we came to the burn. To get across it from the bank and up the other end, Sesky must have made a huge jump, and I lost my balance and fell off. The jump judge asked me if I felt all right, but as Sesky had thankfully stopped just nearby, I thought I was fine and just got back on her, then carried on round the course.

Once we'd safely crossed the finish line, I kept asking the judges and everybody else if I had finished the course. Had we done it? It was only when I went with Sesky to the lorry, tied her up, and went to get an ice pack for her from the First Aid team, that I was stopped and told that I might have suffered concussion from my fall.

As I did not want to go to hospital to be checked, I was eventually driven home – even though I insisted that I felt fine – leaving Sesky, the children, and the lorry behind, to be brought back after me. Not a good end to that day.

I remember I did have a bit of a sore head that night, but I can't recall much more about the actual cross-country course! However, I later learned that we did finish, so it was all worthwhile! Even being unseated once more didn't matter, as I knew we would have thoroughly enjoyed our day, and Sesky was all right, too.

Sesky and me doing our cross-country competition.

By the end of that summer, we'd had a busy time with shows and everything else going on, and the Gleniffer Braes cross-country seemed to come around quicker than expected. This time, when we walked the course, everything looked bigger than before, but I just kept telling myself it was only the novice course. Iona and I had been joking about it for some time, and she'd bet me I would not do it, so I was even more determined that I would.

On the day, off Sesky and I went. Body protector on, mounted on Sesky, I was ready. I had the horsepower, now I just needed to keep the nerves at bay.

I think I must have shut my eyes at most of the jumps – or maybe it just felt like that. I had a good few wobbly ones around the course, and a refusal or two at first, but I managed to stay on and kept going, jumping everything that was there. I must have had Super Glue on my saddle that day.

I remember that whole course, all the way round – four miles, and 25 jumping obstacles. We'd briefly almost got lost in the middle, but I felt that finding our way was our biggest accomplishment to date.

Coming up the hill slope and over the field, slightly out of the saddle, the wind was in my face and the rain dripping off my hat, but Sesky just seemed to pick up the pace. She felt so powerful, comfortable, and in control over this ground, and her jumping just seemed effortless... although that finish line could not come quickly enough for me.

I was ecstatic with Sesky, and it was a wonder she did not run off with the amount of pats and hugs I gave her, along with my favourite words of 'Good girl, Sesky'. When I eventually got off her, once we'd finished and got our breath back, I had the most jelly-like legs you could possibly imagine.

Through time, I did enjoy the cross-country days, but I must admit I found them a bit scary. So, for competition I preferred to stick to showjumping in the arena, whether it was inside or outdoors at the showgrounds or in the fields. Eventually I decided that was the route I was going to go down. After all, we could always ride in the fields at home and, if the urge came, even jump that old fishing boat and burn.

The unaffiliated shows were great fun. Mari-Claire was always on hand to remind me of any jump-off course, as she was a little master at this, although I was so excited about jumping clear in the first round that I could never remember this! To my delight, Sesky nearly always went out and jumped double clear.

Coming home with her rosettes always put a smile on my face. Some days we did not get a rosette, but it was still enjoyable – even on the days I would come out of the arena and the children would tell me I looked 'a bit white' while I was trying to catch my breath.

*

One morning, we were heading off to our mixed show at Gleneagles. We had spent hours the night before getting Sesky and the pony ready – plaiting the manes, using the show sheen everywhere, and doing anything and everything else we could to have them looking prim and proper for their first novice dressage and jumping show. We were both feeling a little bit tired, but as usual we were all up at the crack of dawn to load up and set off to the show. The lorry and everything we needed had all been prepared and packed the night before, so we didn't have much left to do… or so we thought.

The youngest of the boys, Michael, was already grumpy-faced because it was early, so he had climbed into the horsebox to snuggle back to sleep on his makeshift bed, with the usual shout of, 'Wake me up when we get there' as he clambered in, dragging his jacket behind him. Some sweets and money always kept him going at the shows and out of trouble, as he would play about with other children who were there, coming back when he needed more supplies. He was always about to sneak a peek when we jumped, then would quickly disappear again, as we found out.

The pony was put onto the lorry first, because Sesky was going to be first off for her novice dressage class. She came out of her stable looking a million dollars, with her mane beautifully plaited and not a hair out of place; shining, oiled hooves; booted to above the knees to keep her sparkling legs clean; and rugged up to keep her gleaming dapple-grey coat protected while travelling on the lorry. At least, that was the plan.

The first attempt to get her on did not go well, and the second was a total disaster! Sesky pushed off down the ramp, ran through the courtyard, over the car park area and jumped the gate into the wet, muddy field. I could have cried; my worst nightmare had begun.

I remember watching her gallop away, the lead rope dangling from her neck, and the wet and mud splashing everywhere as she ran about enjoying herself. She even had the cheek to eventually stop in the field, snort while looking over at us, and then run off again.

If that was not bad enough, hearing the voices of the children saying, 'Yuk, Mum' in pure disgust, was ten times worse! The job of having to catch Sesky, get her on the lorry, and then clean her, was just not worth thinking about.

It took quite some time, and several attempts and helpful hands, but eventually Sesky was on that lorry with the ramp up. I reversed the lorry around the wall and off we drove. There was not a noise out of them in the back; Sesky was probably too tired from all her running about!

All the way to the show at Gleneagles, I kept thinking about how beautiful she had looked that morning thanks to all our hard work the night before, and then she'd had to go and jump into that field. It would not have been so bad if she had just run off the lorry as normal, but not Sesky… she had to jump into that muddy field!

Also going through my mind on that drive was how many hours I had spent learning my dressage test for this show. It would be Sesky's first dressage test, and for weeks I'd placed the test sheet on the window ledge to study as I made breakfast, lunch, and dinner, reading it through, and through, and through. It was there as I washed the dishes and I read it; it was there as I ironed; I had it in and out of my pocket, reading it, as I worked in the yard mucking out and feeding; I'd read it over and over and over at every hour I could. Now my mind was a jumble, and I couldn't even remember the first part of it, except to enter at A (a marking in the arena). That day really hadn't started the way I'd thought, or hoped, it would.

Arriving at the show, I was dreading taking that back door down to see what disaster stood behind it. First, we would all have a hot roll and tea while we were walking to register for the show and check the class start lists.

As we always left early, or tried to – especially if Sesky was going – I reckoned we still had time to do our classes… until I opened that door of the lorry.

There stood Sesky, with the dirtiest looking face, not to mention the half rubbed-out plaits, munching away quite happily on her hay. When the inner doors were opened, the full picture could be seen of my now filthy horse! The dirt had even seeped through the rug, and her coat was filthy underneath. Somehow, she always found the muddiest, wet bit of the field to run through.

The pony now had to come off first, as the class order had been changed. So, Sesky came off and stood while the pony came off, but amazingly Sesky just went straight back on. *Why could she not have gone on like that this morning?* I groaned to myself.

I now had time to try and clean and wash Sesky off in the back of the lorry while my daughter was warming up and in-between her classes, and eventually Sesky was as clean as she was going to be that day. As I did not have time to re-plait her, the rest of the plaits were taken out and she was left with a curly mane, which would just have to do. I spent the rest of the time reading over the dressage test a few times until it was Sesky's time.

She did not look anything like she had first thing that morning, but as it was raining where I had to warm up and the surface made the horses' legs a bit dirty as they cantered, she looked good enough to go inside to the dressage arena without having to explain what she had done earlier!

To my relief, someone was available to read the test out if you required this, so I went with that option, just to be safe. For Sesky's first dressage novice test, she did not too badly, and with a bit of tail swishing and resistance, we finally got through it.

The best part of the day was later, when the jumping classes were held. Sesky jumped her little heart out as normal, and so did the pony, so the day finished on a good note. Once they were loaded – and she surprisingly just walked on – they began munching again quite happily in the back of the lorry, while we enjoyed a cup of hot soup and food before setting off on our long drive home.

Our first dressage show, Gleneagles, 1992.

One or two more dressage tests were done at the shows with Sesky, and although these were improving, it was just not our thing. I think what finally made up my mind to stop was when we were at one of the shows where the judge's car used to sit at the ringside. Sesky nearly reversed into it while doing her rein back steps and had suddenly thrown in an unplanned change of direction! Sesky was probably thinking, *That's what I think of this dressage!* She went beautifully around the outside of the arena warming up, but as soon as she went in to start the dressage test, as always the tail swishing and the head started, and I knew her marks would not be good even though her transition work and the rest seemed fair. I think probably Sesky made up her mind not to do the dressage before I did!

All set for a dressage show.

Another competition we competed in for a year or two was the Working Hunter class at a local annual agricultural show. Here, Sesky really came into her own, as she had always enjoyed the cross-country in the past, so these jumps were more to her liking than the dressage arena.

The first time we attended this show, Sesky would not load onto the lorry that morning. She'd been good at going on and off for months, but that morning it was just not to be. I decided we were not going to mess about with her, and as I was determined not to miss the show, I opted to hack her along the road a few miles to the showground. Luckily, this one was nice and local to us.

To the surprise of the family, and everyone on the yard at the farm at the time, off I went. Just as with the Gleneagles show, Sesky was looking great and was gleaming as she came out of her stable. The show saddle cloth was on, I was wearing my show jacket and white jodhpurs, as she was also participating later in the other jumping classes, and my entry number was tied round me so I would not lose it. We were ready.

Sesky being good out on the roads made such a difference to our hack. But as this was the first time she would have gone so far along the busy main road, I had left in plenty of time. I wanted to ensure we could have a bit of a rest once we reached the show, and also in case anything happened on our journey.

We got a lot of funny looks that morning as we rode along the road, and a few waves from people who knew us – as well as some who didn't. We enjoyed our hack along, and managed quite a few trots, otherwise we would never have made it.

Our timing, though, was perfect. Despite a few funny looks from the people on the gate, who eventually let us in when I explained what had happened and showed them my competition number, we made it just in time for the first junior jumping class.

Sesky had a rest on the lorry, where surprisingly again she just walked on, and had a munch of hay later then stood quite happily until it was her time to start the

Working Hunter class. After a short warm up, she put in an amazing performance, jumping as if she had done it for years. Everyone commented on her, and in the end she finished fourth. I was delighted, as we'd been up against some good-looking horses that were more experienced than Sesky at jumping this type of class.

Maybe hacking to the show had been the perfect warm up, and had made us more determined to do well!

That day ended on a good note for all of us, with the pony also taking home a few rosettes. At the end of the day, Sesky ran up the ramp into the lorry to be taken home. I guess she did not fancy hacking back along the road again! Whether she had learned a lesson or not, only time would tell.

Sesky jumping her Working Hunter class.

But it was yet another thing we had both accomplished.

Mari-Claire and I went to a lot of shows together over the years, and I distinctly remember returning from one unaffiliated showjumping competition with the horse and pony, cups, medals, and rosettes each. We had a huge smile on our faces that day, as we'd won quite a few jumping classes each, and Sesky had won one of the

Working Hunter Championships. It was certainly a day to remember.

Our last unaffiliated show with a winner's rosette.

It was at that point that Iona and I decided it was time to affiliate Sesky with the British Showjumping Association (BSJA). By that stage, we had competed in and won quite a few unaffiliated shows, or at least jumped double clear. Affiliation with the BSJA would give Sesky and me more of a challenge, and allow us both to progress further.

I always liked a challenge, and this meant that a new chapter in showjumping for Sesky and I was about to begin!

Initially, it meant that one weekend would be spent at unaffiliated shows for the pony, and one weekend at BSJA shows for Sesky. But this only happened for a few months, as Mari-Claire soon affiliated to BSJA, too. That made it so much easier for picking the mixed shows or having turn about. And yes, another pony soon followed.

The horsebox was beginning to feel easier to drive than my Jeep, and reversing was no longer a problem, although I did wonder why Michael still always hid behind the driver's seat while I was manoeuvring, and I'd hear the words 'Oh no!' being muttered behind me!

That couple of years had been really busy, both taking part and enjoying the shows, combined with doing a lot of work at the farm.

Chapter 5

Mixing Business with Pleasure

Part of the yard had been converted to a small livery within the old barn, with stables having been built to house livery clients. Other jobs were also ongoing, including making the other side of the barn into an indoor riding school, and storage for the hay and straw.

As we had all the facilities and land, my idea to run a riding school seemed a good one. With Iona's help, and using her notes and lessons, I started studying for my British Horse Society (BHS) exams. It seemed the perfect way to combine my hobby with work, and enjoy it at the same time.

I also dropped a little hint to Jim the farrier about what I was thinking of doing, just to see if he would be able to take on some extra work if needed. Now the seed was sown, as they say!

Through time, I attended night classes at my favourite place, Gleneagles, which were held for a few hours each time. It involved a one-hour lecture, one hour of theory, and one hour riding. This seemed the best way to fit my studies around the children, as they would be fed and settled before I headed off to my course, leaving them to be looked after as I made the long drive of over an hour to get there, and then the same back again. It was tiring, but it was worth all the effort in the end.

I just wanted to teach, to give people lessons, and the opportunity to ride and enjoy the experience that I'd had with Sesky.

With Iona on hand if I needed her, my lessons carried on at Gleneagles fortnightly over a period of a few months, before I sat my BHS Level 1 exam. My experience on the course also helped me with schooling Sesky, as the group of horses that we were taught on had much more experience. And even at the Level 1 stage, I could feel the difference in these well-schooled horses. I looked forward to riding and jumping them as I worked through my stages with the exams.

I was well used to juggling things about, and organising the children and working from home prior to moving to the farm, so I was pretty sure I could develop the riding school idea and make a go of it.

A few months later, I passed the Level 1 exam and signed straight up for the next stage, along with the BHS Riding & Road Safety exam, and anything else that went with it.

I remember one funny thing about this Level 1 exam, which has provided plenty of laughs with friends over the years. I always use a combination of learning techniques (of my own) while studying. So, if I found it difficult to remember things, I would associate it with something to give me a reminder. And usually, it worked. But this time, on the exam, it did not quite go to plan!

On learning and studying the parts of the horse's leg, I could not for the life of me remember the name for the horny growth on the inside of each leg. This is called the chestnut, but as you will find out later… it also meant something else.

My idea was that I would associate it with the 'acorn'. And although this comes from the oak tree, which is a favourite of mine (and also relates to something completely different), it would remind me of the chestnut. Well…

All the group members were on our first exam and a little shy to answer aloud all the open questions, but when the BHS Examiner pointed to a part of the horse's leg and asked what it was, I said quickly and loudly, 'An acorn.' Immediately I could have sunk into the ground, then quickly added, 'Oh no, I mean a chestnut.' I was dying with embarrassment, but at least it broke the tension in the group. And we all had a bit of a giggle with the examiner about it, particularly when I said I had just been testing!

While working through the grades, the poor livery clients – and everyone and anyone – were used as the guinea pigs as I trained for my teaching exam. But it all helped, and I finally gained the qualification I had worked so hard for.

Sesky and I still had all our riding days, and participated at a good few BSJA Shows, where I was a lot more confident through my riding and jumping experience with the horses at Gleneagles. Sesky went on to jump round her courses with ease, and started collecting her double clear rounds in the British Novice Classes, and then the Discovery Classes. Iona, who was always at the shows with her own horses, would hear me say, 'I think I'll do this one today,' to which she would reply, 'Why not do two? You're here anyway.' So off I would go and enter for the next class.

I must admit it was a lot easier if we were at a horse show, because when it was mixed with horses and ponies, you would end up running from ring to ring. Sometimes, I would be jumping in one ring, while Mari-Claire would be jumping in the next ring at the same time, passing each other at the end of the arenas where they met. Needless to say, she would be jumping her little 12'2 pony a lot higher than I was jumping Sesky in the British Novice Class!

Most of the time, the days went well, though they were always much longer than we anticipated. The weekends going to either horse or pony shows were always busy, as we had to get the horsebox loaded the night before and everything ready, including the horse or pony.

Finally, the riding school was opened in early 1994, and the first pony that I bought was a little black mare named Buttons. A small dainty 12'hh pony, if she were even that, I'd seen her at a yard when I was attending a show. When she came off the lorry for the first time, Sesky was snorting and peering out of her window opening at Buttons, probably thinking this was a little foal.

Michael took a real shine to Buttons, too. Even though he could not ride, he'd spent lots of time around the lessons and watching and being at shows, so he made up his mind he was going to try it out properly for himself this time. Within a few months of Buttons being on the yard, he decided one night after school to tell the girls on the yard that I had said Buttons was to be tacked up for him.

Taking Buttons with him, he disappeared to the field, opened the gate, jumped on the pony, and kicked and kicked… then took off across the field! I had just come up the yard and was shocked to see him, but thankfully he never fell off. Buttons, being a great little pony, had looked after him, but she'd certainly had her cobwebs blown off that day!

He never looked back after that, and became totally smitten with Buttons. Considering that night was his first time on the pony, he did really well, heading across the fields – with a few canters thrown in – with the biggest grin on his face, which made it that bit harder to tell him off. It's a night I will never forget, and I think he won't either.

We went on to bring in a few extra horses and ponies to ensure there was a selection for the riders to fit on and be taught on, and as a result my teaching days became busier and Jim's farrier days grew longer. I don't think he knew what he had let himself in for once the school opened.

The horses and ponies that were field-kept were brought in early, groomed clean on most days when required, and particularly their legs and hooves dried off extra on the days awaiting Jim's arrival. Then, as I listened to him work away, they were changed over quickly for him to carry on.

One day, not long after buying a few new ones, I got them all in early from the field and groomed up, hoof oil on. I was admiring them all as they stood in the corridor munching their hay, ready for their lessons later that day. But my heart sank as Jim drove into the back of the barn, jumped out of the van, looked at the ponies, and said, 'Who on earth put that hoof oil on?!' I had totally forgotten he was coming in that day at ten o'clock to shoe them, so I had to quickly run and get a towel and wipe all the oil off… still not admitting that it was me that had done it So, Jim, when you read this, you will know it was me. Sorry about that. A quick cup of tea and as many biscuits as he wanted were on hand to appease him that morning.

After time, I got to know Susan through the Trekking & Riding Society of Scotland (TRSS). Another idea of mine was to have a Trekking Centre, to allow people to ride outside and away from the arenas. After some research and more discussions, I became interested in pursuing this idea, and attended a few courses for further training.

Some of the courses were for a full week, and involved staying on-site to do the training and be assessed before sitting an exam at the end of the week. The training involved everything from catching the horses and ponies from the field on incredibly early mornings, to stable management, and from riding the hills, burns, forests, and jumping the odd fallen tree, to finding our way back to the yard. I'm afraid compass reading was never my greatest thing! This was an enjoyable way to learn everything, and although it was good experience riding different-sized horses and ponies, I missed not having Sesky with me.

I trotted on (you could say) for the next year or two, running the school and trekking, passed various exams through the TRSS, and became qualified for my Centre Operator's Certificate, and later my British Equestrian Tourism Qualification. I also gained my Diploma in Equestrian Tourism, which is my greatest achievement. I remember being so pleased to know that if anything went wrong when out on a trek, I should be knowledgeable enough to deal with it. Even though my treks did not go over hills and moors, like the ones we did in training, they could still be quite challenging, especially as most of the time the people were tourists with a lot of varied riding ability and experience – or none!

Most of the treks were either out across the special path which we had made between the fields, or over the open fields, then up the mostly quiet country roads. The more advanced riders would tackle crossing the main road, then go along the dirt tracks where you could get the most beautiful view of the loch, then meet up with the quieter country roads, canter back in across the open fields, and enjoy a leisurely walk along the trekking path back to the yard.

Sesky and I had ridden all the routes, measured them out, timing all the different trot spots, walking and canter parts, and the preparation work proved to be so much fun. I loved making the longer routes for the experienced riders, and allowing for adjustments within the times for anything that might go wrong. I was determined to have that Plan B in my head, which could be thrown in without the riders knowing if I had to adjust the treks unexpectedly, or if the riders turned out not to manage the route for any reason. There was also the possibility that any of the horses and ponies might unexpectedly play up with their rider, so a trek would not go to plan.

On some occasions, we would just be walking over the dirt tracks or around the country roads, when the odd dog would run out and bark at us, startling the horses and ponies – or that odd pheasant. We just needed to be ready for something out of the blue happening like that. Not all dogs like horses; some may be frightened by the size of the horse, or even just the smell, or just start barking as this strange animal going past.

Dogs have always been part of my family, even when I was a little girl growing up, but the horses and ponies weren't so keen. And the size of the dogs didn't matter –

whether they were as little as Stig, my friend Agnes's dog, or bigger like a good few of our own dogs. If something barked loudly at them, some of the horses or ponies would be frightened. Sesky, thankfully, was used to dogs being about, so she was always there to steady the ride down. And luckily, most of the dogs we met just walked calmly by on the lead while the horses and ponies gave them a wide berth.

When something did frighten them, the riders would be led back by someone either on foot or on their own horse or pony, to help them control their mount if they could not. That was where the trek assistants would come into play. Having been on the courses, passed the exams, and worked my way up through the grades with the TRSS and BHS, I had the knowledge and understanding to pass onto the girls that worked on the yard. And this helped with their training and development over the years.

Despite being busy at the farm, the shows still went ahead, with Sesky and me – along with my daughter and her pony – working our way up through the grades in different classes.

Sesky had been jumping well with the BSJA, and had qualified for one or two of the Second Round Competitions, some of which were held just near the border with England. But as she was not great at going on the lorry at times, and some of the Second Rounds were quite big, I decided not to take part in the ones that were far away. We did, however, compete in one or two of these Second Rounds that were on home ground, but again we just had to have that bit more experience of jumping the bigger tracks above Discovery Class for these.

The jumping practice in the arena at home carried on as it had done in previous years, with the pole being raised each time to encourage Sesky and I to jump that little bit higher. Jumping the Discovery at one metre seemed easy enough, and the jump-off was not too bad, being up that bit higher. But the thought of jumping the Newcomers Class round the whole track, at one metre ten, was a little bit harder for me to swallow. *And what if we jumped clear?* I worried. *Then we would need to do the jump-off, which would be higher again.* That fear was enough to make me think again.

We were now out of the British Novice Class, after winning the total amount of prize money allowed for that section, which meant Sesky and I only then had the Discovery Class in which to jump. I had always used the British Novice as my warm-up for the Discovery Class, so that left me with a problem. But, as luck would have it, the good old one-metre class that appeared in some shows could be used for our warm-up for the Discovery.

The placings were a lot harder to get at these shows, as over the bigger tracks I just had not managed to connect the speed for the jump-off with going clear. So, for a while we gathered steady double clear rounds rather than winning rosettes. Then, through time, we did get that rosette – but not always at the top end of the line-up. The bonus, though, was that remaining within the prize money winnings limit meant Sesky could stay in the Novice Classes, which was great for picking up the jumping experience.

One summer, we not only won the red first place rosette in one of the Novice Classes at the show, but Sesky also won the small cup and sash to go with it. *Good girl, Sesky*, I thought, as our names would now go on the trophy.

Our first attempt at jumping the Newcomers Class – one metre ten – was at one of the winter indoor shows. I had jumped the Discovery Class with Sesky, and after jumping double clear, I was sitting in the seating area with Iona having coffee, when she asked why we didn't want to try the Newcomers Class that day. I nearly choked on my coffee and immediately dismissed the idea, but when she jokingly challenged that I was 'probably scared', and we had a laugh, I changed my mind. Truthfully, I *was* scared, but nevertheless I marched to the entries area and submitted our names to jump our first Newcomers Class.

When I told the children what we were doing, their expressions of disbelief said it all. Michael just mumbled, 'Guess we are not leaving now then,' as he clambered down over the seats, then disappeared with the other children at the show, with a few pounds in his hand for the burger van or some sweets.

The next thing I knew we were course walking, then off to get tacked up again. The hardest job for me was to remember the course, as I was too concerned at the height of the full course never mind where all the jumps were. After watching quite a few other riders jump the course, I then had to get on Sesky and warm up. The thought of going into that arena to jump filled me with trepidation, but soon it was our turn. In we went… and before I knew it, we had completed the full course – and jumped clear! I could now breathe.

We were all so pleased, and Sesky had jumped her little heart out again. But the thought of having to tackle even bigger in the jump-off and against the clock – even after that steady clear round – was making me have second thoughts. After careful consideration, I decided I would leave the jump-off this time, and not attempt it. I always like to finish on a good note, and I did not reckon participating in the jump-off would be that. At least our first Newcomer competition was out of the way, and we could try a jump-off another day.

Over the next few months, we jumped a good few Newcomer Classes, and if Sesky did jump clear, we attempted the jump-off. Some attempts were better than others, but I felt I was getting out of my comfort zone and having to face bigger jumps than I liked.

The indoor and outdoor shows came and went as the months flew past, and the horsebox clocked up plenty of miles going to all the different venues. We had so much fun, and no matter the weather, we would be loaded up and off we would go.

At one show we attended, the warm-up and the Newcomers classes were jumped, with one unlucky pole falling in the first round. Sesky had felt amazing that day from the minute I had sat on her, jumping round the Newcomers comfortably and looking rather pleased with herself.

Then Iona just had to say, 'I dare you to jump the Foxhunter. It doesn't look as big a course today, and not much different to what you've just jumped.'

I nearly fell off my seat. 'You are joking,' I remember saying, and there were a few words exchanged, then off I marched to enter the class. I was convinced that it was a waste of money even participating, but didn't want to be defeated, so I sank my fears and got ready. 'I can do this,' I mumbled to myself as I mounted Sesky.

The practice jumps were fine, but a bit of a hit or a miss, you might say. Then the clear one came, and off we went.

I remember seeing the children standing at the side of the arena, almost covering their faces as I went past them. Basically, everything after that seemed to disappear, apart from the Foxhunter Course. *What was I doing?*

The jumping round was touch and go, then there was a line of white gates through the diagonal centre. I must have just kicked and grabbed on, and before I knew it, we were out the other side, leaving them standing, and finishing the course – demolishing a few jumps as we went round!

I just remember saying, 'Eat your heart out Devon Leisure,' as I left the indoor arena. The children ran over to see us, and Sesky got lots of 'well done' pats that day.

We never attempted a Foxhunter class again, but at least we had tried one. As there was still plenty of space in Sesky's prize money winnings for the Newcomers, this is where she stayed.

Most weekends, I must admit, the one-metre class or the one-metre-ten class is what we did, only participating in the Newcomers on a good day, because it just always looked that bit bigger.

But every day was a good day riding Sesky, wherever we were.

The shows continued for us, and the junior shows were busy, too. We would decide on which ones we would attend, and obviously if the junior shows had qualifiers, we'd head there. Sesky would be left at home if it was not a mixed show, as it was an important one for Mari-Claire and the pony.

Sesky never seemed to enjoy having a day off, strangely enough. The next day she would always be grumpy for about the first ten minutes or so while riding, and I would not even waste my time trying to correct her. I would just let her run round at her pace in walk and trot, grumping about until her tantrum was over, then she would settle down and the schooling would start. I guess Sesky just loved her work and had the stamina to keep going. Maybe I should have tried Endurance Riding with her!

The Riding School and Trekking Centre was getting busier, and different horses and ponies had been brought in. The odd one or two, we later found out by surprise, were in foal – something we hadn't realised when they were bought from the dealers' yard.

The first horse that we got from the dealers' yard turned out to be in foal, months after she arrived. The foal was born one early misty morning, and was curled up beside her mum that morning when I had gone out. Forgetting that it was still incredibly early, I was so excited that I ran into the house shouting for everyone to wake up and come and see little Misty, as I named her.

Then there was a little pony who arrived a few months later and had to go into the isolation stables, with coming in new. Within weeks, there was a little foal in the stable early one morning. It was so small and dainty – its mother being a 12'2 pony – and was the cutest little foal I had ever seen. I even wondered if the old gate on the stable would be low enough to stop the foal from rolling underneath it, so we bedded the gate all round with straw to make sure it would be safe. As the mum was called Fudge, it was decided by the children that the foal would be called Toffee.

You might think we would have learned from the experience of having two 'surprise' foals, but it happened again a few years later. We bought a lovely little 14' pony from the dealers, and had her working away in the school for a few months without realising she was pregnant. After the lessons were finished, we always turned out the horses and ponies in the field. One morning, I went down into the field early, and thought a calf had got through from the other field and was at the ponies. But when I got closer, I realised it was a little black foal. I thought I was dreaming!

Immediately, I ran up the fields to the house to shout and wake everybody up again, to come and see this foal! Then we had the job of getting the new foal and its mum away from all the other ponies and into a stable.

You might laugh, but I was not the only one that hadn't noticed the pony had been in foal. The vet had been up to check her a few weeks earlier about a growth under her tail, which had been annoying her when being ridden in the school for lessons. As the pony was otherwise looking extremely healthy, bright, and a good weight, nothing apart from the growth had been checked, and there had been no mention that she might be in foal.

I could not wait to phone the vet that morning to tell him that I had found more than a growth under her tail – this time, the growth was a foal! Not long after the call, he came up to the yard and saw the foal for himself. 'I'll be damned,' he commented, taking his skipped hat off, shaking his head and laughing. We all had a good chuckle that morning, especially when I admitted I had been wondering where the foal had come from!

The other thought that had gone through my head was that the birth meant we had one pony less to use in the riding school for a while, but at least our recent purchase had provided us with two for the price of one!

This little foal soon proved to be the quickest little mover there ever was. He used to fly about the yard, well ahead of his mother, while going to the field, and bouncing and jumping anything that got in his way. Even though he was small, he would jump out over the stable door when any horse or pony walked past. He was a real handful, and we named him Jet.

Those days were busy with teaching in the school, trekking out, and attending more shows on the junior showjumping circuit with a few ponies. But the little foals always provided something to watch, and briefly took our busy minds off everything else.

Through the months and years of having the little foals, the idea came into my head about breeding Sesky, who was now nine years old. Perhaps I could produce a horse for showjumping in the future?

As she'd had a foal before she came to me, I thought this could be a great idea, and I decided to put her into foal. It wasn't long before Sesky was scanned in foal, and for me the next eleven months could not pass quickly enough. With a showjumping stallion having been used, I was excited to think how her little foal would turn out.

I still rode Sesky almost every day, but only on light rides as time went on. We would go out quite happily together, round the country roads which she loved across the fields, or just in the school for a bit. As she still thrived on her work, it kept her nice, fit, healthy, and in good condition.

The months were busy, and Sesky kept well through her pregnancy. One day, when she was about seven months pregnant, we were hacking across the fields and I decided not to take our usual route up the roads. Instead, I allowed Sesky just to wander where she wanted around the fields. I think that was the day Sesky decided she was ready for a break from riding. I just had that feeling, which comes from knowing your horse and both having that special connection.

So, her saddle and bridle were cleaned and stored away for a while, and her lazier days began, just going out to the field and coming back in when she was ready. Sesky was never the best horse at being caught from the field, so it was a waste of time even trying. Many times over the years she had taken off with the lead rope while we were trying to catch her. It was easier, instead, to wait and she would come to the gate and stand when she was ready to come in.

With Sesky getting quite wide and big, the entrance into her own stable in the courtyard opposite the house was becoming a bit too neat for her to turn in and around. It was then that her stable had to be moved up the yard.

The old bull pens that had originally been at the back of the other barn, had been made into stables, and the size of these were ideal for foaling boxes. They also had an open back halfway up, where the wall was inside the barn, which was ideal for Sesky to look over and down to the house. It meant she could still see me as I came out of the house, and she would neigh as usual as I called out, 'Good girl, Sesky.'

When I'd walk past the barn, she would pop out over her front stable door on the other side, and patiently wait for me to walk round to her. She always liked to see what was going on and what I was up to, and expected me to go over to her – which I always did. During those final months of her pregnancy, I was continually checking on her. I could not wait for the foal to be born.

And I was not the only one who was excited. We had lots of tourists riding, along with our weekly clients, so Sesky's impending birth became a regular topic of conversation.

Sesky in foal, at the back of her stable, 1997.

She loved being patted by everyone and watching them milling about. But when she'd had enough of being 'visited', she made it quite clear by standing at the back of her stable and refusing to come near the door. Not even for a carrot! She was quite a character.

Jim was kept busy shoeing with the school – as was Alison, taking the phone calls – and some days he would be with us from early morning until well after lunchtime. Tea and a snack were thrown in to keep him sweet, especially when we were joined by the trekking horses – the 'heavy team', as I called them.

I always made sure Sesky got done first and out of the way before they were shod. Although Jim liked to stand back and admire the trekking horses once they were finished, I always felt that Sesky was his favourite. On one occasion, he even rode her in the school when he was preparing for going to a show to judge the riding class. He was a qualified BHS instructor – something that also came in handy at times.

Jim also got me one of my favourite little ponies, Smokey, as he knew someone who was selling her. She was a godsend, and I used to think she was a little lookalike to Sesky. Jim and Alison would bring their young daughter up to the school many times, and he would give her a lesson on Smokey or just a shot on a pony.

As we had become so busy with the riding school and trekking, and having more horses and ponies, I took the decision to close the small livery yard. It meant that the evenings were quiet times for the horses and ponies once lessons were finished, with just the children playing about riding or on the quad bikes. For me, it was nice to have some grooming time with Sesky, and to spoil her. Michael had even got his own pony, named Seven, and was having fun with him over little jumps. Being an older school master, this was ideal for him. I used to wonder if he would be joining his sister and me at the shows, and he did do so later for a bit.

CHAPTER 6

NEW BEGINNINGS

Waiting for Sesky to foal seemed like the longest eleven months ever. I kept wishing the winter months to be over so we could reach spring and the arrival of the new foal.

The days and nights of checking her seemed to go on forever. Then one morning in April, Sesky's little foal made its appearance during the early hours – and I just missed it! After all the hours of peeping in on her when I knew she was due to foal, she had held on until she was ready and no-one was around to watch. Only the little cats that were hanging around the stable must have been there! I did what I always did. With sheer delight, I ran down to the house, shouting all the way that Sesky had had her foal. Then, without even waiting on a reply, I ran back up again.

I opened the stable door quietly and went in, patting Sesky lovingly, then I moved to the corner to watch.

The little foal was scrambling to its feet, trying to stand, but falling forward and back down onto its nose as it tried to balance itself. Sesky neighed softly and licked it, and when the foal stumbled to the ground, she nudged it gently as if to say, 'I will help you.'

I moved over to fix the straw round about, and could see we had a little filly foal. The foal kept attempting to get up, then falling, standing for a second then collapsing back down again, but she would not give up. Then, with one almighty push up, she stood wobbling as if on a tightrope trying to balance, and eventually fell towards Sesky.

With her mother's encouragement, she scrambled again, and this time made it up, balanced against Sesky, then made her way underneath and, with a few nudges from Mum, latched on and began drinking. After she'd managed enough to satisfy her, the little foal flopped down on the straw and nestled beside Sesky then went to sleep. It was now rest time for Sesky and the foal, and after giving them a check over with a loving pat and feeling of accomplishment, I quite happily left them, whispering 'Good girl, Sesky' as I shut the stable door behind me.

The little, nearly black, filly foal was adorable, and both she and Sesky were well. Even though she was quite protective at first, Sesky did not seem to mind us going into have a closer look and cuddle later that morning. What a super mum she was, and having had a foal previously, she was a natural.

The difference in just an hour or two was amazing to witness. Now, when the foal got up, she jumped to her feet, moved quickly to Sesky for a drink, then flew excitedly around the stable with little jumps in the air. Sesky would neigh at her, and the foal would whimper back, and it was just incredible to watch them together. I had waited so long for this moment, and now it was playing out right in front of my eyes!

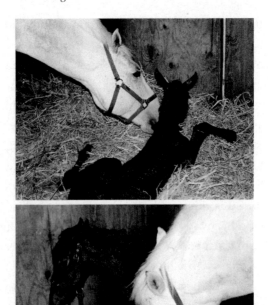

Sesky with her foal, April 1997.

I think I spent most of my time at their stable for the next few weeks, and virtually had to be dragged from their side. With someone else around to help with teaching, I was able to devote my time to Sesky and her foal. With an adorable white star marking on her head, it seemed appropriate for us to call her Star.

The other foals that were born on the yard had grown up fast, and Star was our little youngster. Toffee was now a yearling, and Misty, at two years old, was maturing into a lovely little horse.

Sesky just loved to stand and be groomed while munching away at her hay, and the little foal was quite happy to sniff about me as I was grooming her mum. The foal got a little brush if she stood still for maybe five minutes, then she'd dart off, pushing under Sesky to get some milk.

Many a day she would flee around the stable as I was mucking them out, which proved to be a difficult task on the days they could not go out to the field. It was so much easier when they were turned out and I had peace to do the stable properly and make up that lovely big bed for them coming back in. The foal used to love dodging under the straw as it was put down for them.

The field gate, which was next to Sesky's stable, was good for turning them out, and handy for getting them in. Sometimes, when we used the further away gate to the field, Sesky would pull round to make sure the foal was there, as it was running and jumping around and making her quite anxious.

One of the most amazing moments was when they first came out of the stable together, and the foal was turned out into the big open world. The foal whimpered loudly for her mum as they went into the field, but Sesky ran ahead then stopped and remembered she had a foal, before then neighing, and looking for her. She gave Star a few nudges as she came beside her, as if to tell her to stay there, then quite happily munched away at the grass as Star fed off her.

It was lovely to see Sesky's bound for freedom that morning, and the foal standing over Sesky as she had a roll in the grass, pawing the ground as if she wanted her mother to get up again. And it never fails to amaze me how foals can run so fast when they are only days old.

The hard part of having Sesky and Star now was going away to the junior shows at the weekend, and leaving them behind. Although the girls were working on the yard, I always looked forward to getting back and seeing Sesky and the foal, and to find out what they had been up to during the day. As soon as the other ponies were unloaded, I would go in to Sesky and spend some time with her, and watch this little addition spring about the stable.

That seemed to be quite a quick year, as we were busy with the school, shows, and with Michael often competing in the Novice Classes on his little pony, Seven. I was also engrossed with Star growing and maturing over the months. Although we'd had other foals, this one seemed different, but she probably just seemed special because she was Sesky's.

Sesky was great at being a mum again, and she and Star would just walk in and out to the field with no problems; getting them both back in was becoming quite easy, too. With Star being handled and leading, she was good to catch, and on the odd occasion when Sesky did not want to co-operate, all we had to do was walk away with Star with a bucket of feed, and her mother would soon follow.

One thing Sesky did not like was when she was in the field with Star, and I was riding or walking along with the treks with the other horses and ponies. She would run up and snatch at them over the fence, and then gallop off, bucking in the air, chasing Star with her. I guess she was just being protective. It was quite funny to watch, as she would then stand near the middle of the field with Star and look over to us all, nudging the foal as if to tell her to stay well away from us. This actually became a talking point with the tourists we took out riding.

And often, before the clients left, they'd be lucky enough to have Sesky and Star come over to receive a pat.

On the occasions when they returned from their trek to find Sesky and Star were back in their stable, they could see them over the door. But if Sesky was not in the best mood and snapped over the door at them, I'd go over and urge the visitors to look from a distance, and hopefully get a glance of Star jumping about inside.

Sesky was always super with the farrier, even from the first day I got her, and she was still quite young. And once Star came along and Jim the farrier was trimming Sesky's feet, I'd ask him to pick up Star's feet, too, and pretend to be working on her hooves. It was a great way to get her used to the farrier, although at the start there was a bit of jumping about. Maybe he smelled a bit different, with the farrier smoke with shoeing, so she wasn't sure, but she got used to him over time and eventually didn't bother at all. Her little face trying to jump up at the door while Sesky was outside getting her feet done, was quite funny to see.

I always found it really rewarding to handle the foals from the start and get them used to different things they would have to deal with when they were older. This included, in time, being loaded onto the horsebox, stood to be fed a treat, and taken back off. This would be done regularly, as I did not want them not loading, or taking off the ramp as Sesky had always done. So, on a quiet day we would just load them up, then off, with no fuss, in the hope that the experience would get them used to going on and off. And, thankfully, I can't remember Sesky running off the lorry on those days!

Sesky and Star had lots of lovely times together out in the field enjoying each other's company, and cosy days inside when the weather was not good, especially through the winter. As we had the indoor school at the time, it was great to let them both have a run about inside and enjoy some freedom on those bad weather days. Of course, I had to stand guard at the end to ensure that neither of them tried to jump the large gate out!

As time went on, I knew the day would soon come when I would have to separate them. I decided to leave them together that first part of the winter, to enjoy some extra time together, then separate them after the New Year. But even then, I felt so guilty when the time came. Sesky was not amused at all, and as she had to stay on the yard, her loud neighing made her views crystal clear to everyone around! Some days I thought she was going to jump out over the stable door, and the look on her face when I went into see her, just made it clear that she was NOT happy.

On the run-up to the separation, Sesky had spells of time away from Star, often in the school by herself, having a free run about, and for longer periods each time, and neither of them seemed particularly bothered. But not getting Star back was a different story, and Sesky showed her very grumpy side then!

Night times were the worst, and we had to leave the radio playing loudly – and through the night – to drown out the sound of Sesky and Star neighing back and forward to each other. It wasn't so bad during the day, as there was always plenty going on to take their minds off neighing for a while. Sesky, being in her own big foaling stable, was kept to what she was used to, while Star had gone inside the other barn to the stables, with a gate across the top of the door. This was handy for keeping her closed in, and preventing her from trying to jump out over the door. She had rammed at it a few times, but thankfully not hurt herself. Here, she could also see all the other horses and ponies coming and going from their lessons or treks, and all the work going on.

Eventually, as they both settled down over a few weeks, the radio was turned down bit by bit and finally reached a level where you could hear yourself think again. And when the sound finally went back to normal, we still left the radio on during the night as a distraction.

To take her mind off the separation, Sesky was taken out to the field with one of the ponies she liked, but a few times she was still a bit dramatic if she heard Star neigh nearby. After a crazy gallop around the field, though, she'd eventually be distracted by the pony and the lovely, lush grass, and would settle down again. The pony, on the other hand, just stood watching her all the time, as if it was thinking, *Crazy horse!*

Once she was settled in her new stable, Star would be let into the indoor school to have a run around to tire her out, then have the gate above her stable door opened so she could look out into these big new surroundings. As things got better and the odd neigh did not really seem to bother either of them, once Sesky came in from the field and was half asleep at the back of her stable, Star would then go up to the top field paddock with one of the little ponies who would keep her in check. This seemed to work out well, and we would often change the ponies around to keep Star occupied in the field.

When Sesky first came to me – and for a while later – she would herd up any other horses or ponies she was in the field with, as if she was the boss – probably because she had been used to being in a herd in fields for years before coming to me. I was always afraid she might get kicked by other horses, as she was so bossy, and she would always chase them away and not allow anyone to be caught. It was a bit of a nightmare for everyone. After a while, to make things easier and safer for everyone, Sesky was turned out on her own one day to see what she would do – and she never bothered. From then on, it was more convenient for me to put her out on her own. And she clearly enjoyed it better, too.

Rosie, who was one of our novice showjumping ponies, soon became Sesky's friend, and once she got more used to the separation from Star, they spent quite a few months together going out in the field. Then, when Sesky was back to normal, she went back out on her own before she started bossing Rosie about too much. On the days when Rosie went out in the field next to Sesky's stable with the other showjumping ponies, she would come over to the gate to see Sesky leaning out over her stable door, and stand there as if they were having a chat with each other, then she would run off and join the other ponies. A little friendship had grown, and it was really cute to watch.

Rosie was a favourite of Michael's, and although she was his sister's novice jumping pony, he loved to have a shot on her. At a couple of the shows later, as she developed, he could jump her a few times in the odd Novice Classes. They would jump double clear, and he would finish and jump back off her, giving her back to me, then run off to play with his pals while still wearing his white jodhpurs. Rosie was a wonderful pony, and spent a few years with us, giving my son the experience of jumping round – and the odd rosette.

She was a young, beautiful Skewbald mare, a great jumper, and had such a lovely nature. The funniest memory of her was at a show in Aberdeen, when my son got the chance to jump the small Novice Class on her – but it did not all go quite to plan. He had a few mishaps and came out the arena saying, 'It was Rosie. Her steering was not working today,' with a look of disgust as he walked away to play, leaving his sister laughing at him as she was left to deal with the pony!

That year, getting someone in to help with the yard allowed us to travel to a lot of the junior shows all over Scotland, and down to England and Wales. It also meant there was someone more experienced on the yard to help with the teaching, treks, and to handle the youngsters.

Chapter 7

Mindset

One thing I really looked forward to doing was getting Sesky back into being ridden again. After having a few months in and out of the field following her separation from Star, Sesky was brought back into work, and she was loving it as she had before. Our days and nights of hacking out were back, and after the evening teaching night was finished, Sesky and I would head out round our country roads for our special quiet, relaxing time. The two of us alone together – the way we liked it!

That year, it felt as though I had more horses and ponies everywhere. There was such a good selection in the school, and the few youngsters and the odd livery belonging to staff made it such a busy place. There were showjumpers, too, as these ponies had changed a few times as well.

Sesky was changing and becoming a bit lighter than her darker dapple-grey colour. This made the grooming job on her more difficult, as I hated if she even had a stable stain on her. I would clean her up even just to be turned out into the field, which amused the girls on the yard at the time. Of course, just before Sesky would come in from the field, she nearly always managed to find the dirtiest part to roll in, then would stand looking at me at the gate, as if to say 'What?' – and with the dirtiest face ever. Her body was not much better either! Obviously, that meant a thorough grooming was the next job before riding!

As Sesky and I built up our work together again, I realised how much I had missed riding her. Even though I had ridden the school horses and ponies out on the treks while she was off, it was not the same. I missed our time together, our rides out, and coming back when we wanted to from our hack, or even just out of the school. There was nothing better than having the radio turned up and riding in the school in peace, just Sesky and me listening to my favourite tunes, forgetting about the time – and anything else – for a little while. Or hacking out round the lovely countryside and meeting various people – something she loved to do – and receiving lots of loving pats. There were a few favourite old men, women, and children, who would come out every time they saw us coming past, and Sesky would get a little treat while we had a chat. When Sesky decided she had stood long enough and was ready to move, we would carry on for a while then head back home. Time just did not seem to matter.

Sesky and I had a dirt track leading off the country road which became one of our normal points of choice. When we approached it, I would allow Sesky to either turn her head into this track, or if she kept her head straight to the road, that's where we would go! The choice depended on her mood of the day, but she often picked the dirt track when she maybe felt tired, as going round the road was the longer route.

At the beginning, when she was not paying attention and I chose to go straight down the road, our trek around the long route did not go as well. So it became something of a game for us both, and Sesky and I would often disappear together for hours on end.

It became normal practice on the yard that if I was having a bad or hectic day, or the others had had enough of me for the day, they'd groom and tack up Sesky then I'd be told to go off for a hack. I, and they, knew that I would return in a much happier mood. I must admit, it always worked a treat, no matter what time of day or night it was. It was just a totally relaxing way to switch off and live in that moment of peaceful, enjoyable riding time with Sesky.

We'd had a busy year with travelling to the junior circuit of showjumping with three ponies at a time, and a lot of stayaway shows. All the bigger shows and qualifiers were held more often in England than on home ground, and I think my horsebox could have driven down south on its own, as it had been up and down that road so many times. Thank goodness our horseboxes had living accommodation in them by that stage, too.

Having a determined junior rider in Mari-Claire, the shows for the year were immediately marked out on the calendar from 1st January. I used to think watching her compete and ride was like poetry in motion.

It was a year in which Sesky maybe only did a few shows, which were pushed in when nothing else was on, so I had probably become a bit rusty with not competing. On the occasions we did take part, the little Open Novice Class came in handy, as I could jump without worrying too much about the height, and Sesky got a little flavour of what she had missed. It never seemed to bother her about going back in, even though she had only been back into work for a good six months or so by then. And it was lovely that she even went onto the lorry without any real fuss, too. Maybe becoming a mum again had changed her a bit. By the winter, she was back to being her fit young self, comfortably into our normal riding routine, and nothing seemed too much work again.

The following year was a year of reducing the number of horses and ponies in the school, as I realised that buying the odd one or two at the shows over the years had really mounted up! Maybe I got a shock when they were more noticeable all out in the fields next to each other, with their new light blue waterproof rugs on. It certainly showed up the amount we had. I guess that was not a good shopping spree idea!

The showjumpers were being changed over, although one or two of the ponies were kept. Little Rosie was sold on to a lovely family down south, who would have years and years of fun together with this beautiful pony. Michael was sad to see her go – as were we – and he vowed never to ride a horse again after she was sold. He has been almost true to his word, and has only ever been on one since. To this day, I still keep in touch with Linda, Rosie's new owner.

One of the little youngsters, Toffee, was also sold, and with Star being almost two years old, I wondered whether it might be good to have another foal from Sesky. She was now twelve years old, so I was aware I would have to plan it at some point. I was conscious that it would provide us with more, hopefully, showjumping youngsters, and there was also more space now on the yard.

That year, Mari-Claire competed on Sesky, and was making good progress with her in the Novice Classes. She had come off ponies a few years early, and although Sesky was never going to be that big 'Open' jumping horse, she filled the gap for a while just to keep her competing. And if anyone could get a great tune out of a horse, it was certainly my daughter.

Sesky jumped her little heart out, and even on the days she didn't do too well, I still gave her plenty of pats and words of encouragement. They both even won the same cup that Sesky and I had several years before at one of the outdoor summer shows, so I was thrilled that their names were added to it too.

Over the months they collected some good 1st placings, with Sesky being ridden in the jump-off like I had never ridden her before, and she was loving every second of it. Although she was jumping the Novice Classes, and the other classes she took part in were bigger than anything I had jumped clear with her, they had some really good results.

Their biggest achievement was when they qualified for the Stafford Festival in 1999, in the under-16 riders' class. I was thrilled for Mari-Claire, as she had worked so hard with Sesky to qualify. And although she was used to taking part in these type of competitions on the ponies, it was all new to Sesky. The big event was now highlighted on the calendar, and something to look forward to near the end of the year.

Through time I had come across another horse with the same breeding as Sesky, thanks to a friend at one of the shows. As Sesky was such a great hardy little horse, I had told my friend I wanted another similar one, and asked her to keep her eyes open. As this was an opportunity not to be missed, Copper soon came to join us.

Copper, being a great little novice horse, jumped clear most of the time, progressed through her classes with my daughter, and both she and Sesky jumped at many shows together throughout their travels, indoors and out. Many a rosette was brought home by them and hung proudly on the wall, and Sesky and Copper became great friends.

In no time the Stafford Festival was upon us. Having other normal Novice Competition classes at the show meant we could bring another horse along with Sesky. This allowed two horses to compete at the show, which made the long journey worthwhile. We had a day off when we got there, and used the time well to get a good feel for the place ahead of the actual competition. Sesky was not one to bother with fillers at the jumps, or water trays, so I knew that with a good jockey on top, she had a good chance of doing well at jumping in this Under-16 Class final. My only concern was that this big indoor arena, with galleries round about it and so much going on, was nothing that Sesky had ever experienced before.

As they warmed up for the class, the jumping track looked so big to me, but Mari-Claire was not fazed by it at all. When the riders did the course walk, I led Sesky round the collecting ring, giving her a pat and thinking, *You will need to jump your little heart out in there today!* After a few practice jumps, off they went into the arena, leaving me with my heart pounding as I watched from the entrance wall.

I was so nervous that I think I lifted my leg up and jumped every obstacle with them, counting the jump numbers to myself as they made their way around the course. The last jump could not come quickly enough for me, but soon they went through the finish with all the poles still standing. Ecstatic, I jumped in the air. A clear round; eat your little hearts out, Stafford! My little horse had been ridden amazingly, and she had jumped her little legs off. I was so delighted for them both.

The only thing now standing before them was the big jump-off track – and I did not even want to look at it. As she'd jumped many big and Grand Prix tracks with the ponies, I knew that Mari-Claire was well able to tackle the course. *But would Sesky be able to jump it?* I wondered.

The warm-up went as normal, then in they went. If I'd felt nervous before, it was nothing to how I felt then! Sesky jumped the first few fences well, but then some of the course was just not to be, and a few poles fell. It was the biggest course that she had tackled in this setting, and although she did not jump clear, she did as well as a lot of the horses on that day who were probably a lot more experienced at these types of tracks.

I would say that was Sesky's best achievement in her jumping to date, and she had been ridden beautifully as always. The picture of them jumping over the water tray at the Stafford Festival 1999 still hangs on my wall today. It's one of my favourite jumping pictures of Sesky, as she looks like a true professional. A little horse with a big heart. And despite the result, Sesky got lots of those special 'Good girl, Sesky' pats from me that day.

The Stafford Festival was also the place where I saw my favourite stallion jump. I had been watching him competing through the summer months, thinking he would be a good one for Sesky to breed with. I really liked his jumping and everything about him, including his nature. That was an important consideration, because Sesky – as I had found out often in the past – could be pretty strong-willed. As I had already enquired about him and got the price for breeding,

I was still deciding what to do when I watched him take part in the Stafford show. His performance convinced me and, as we both liked him, the decision was made. This would be Sesky's next stallion for breeding – and, as she was almost 14 now, it had to be sooner rather than later.

Despite Stafford being her furthest journey away from home, Sesky had travelled well, and she was back jumping again soon after. When the photographs I'd ordered from the show arrived, I was thrilled, as I could relive that special day time and time again and proudly show them off to everyone at the yard… and everywhere else, too.

The horse shows over the next year were busy, with Sesky going out quite often, jumping with another few horses. Her classes were specially chosen just to keep her happy and not over-fazing her, and thankfully she behaved almost all the time going on and off the lorry.

As we had the other horses for showjumping now, I decided in the springtime that Sesky would be put into foal, particularly as the shows for her were starting to ease off. With the stallion already decided, now the timing would just need to be right for getting her into foal. Hopefully, everything would go to plan.

When August 2000 came around, I had a huge smile on my face when Sesky was scanned in foal! I think I danced around the whole yard that day and all week. Her foal was due in June 2001, and with Sesky normally giving birth near her date, I was determined not to miss this one.

As before, Sesky stayed in work for a while, with me riding her as normal and using her on the trekking rides I took out. I picked the ones I thought would be enjoyable for her, as she was always my great trek-leading horse. On the bigger treks, sometimes we would just change to the back of the ride and allow the assistant to take the front for a while.

Sesky enjoyed the other horses and ponies being out with us, as we walked the line of the trek to chat with the riders. They were always delighted to learn, during conversation, that Sesky was in foal.

On other days, she would spend the morning quite happily in the field in the sunshine, munching the grass, only lifting her head when she saw the treks going in and out with me riding one of the school horses or ponies. This 'time off' kept her nice and fresh for our ride out in the evenings after work was finished – that special time we had together that I always looked forward to.

The riding clients on the treks always liked to pat Sesky when they came back, then have a look at Star, who was now three years old and getting big, along with Misty, who was now over four, and all the others.

Sesky had such a good summer and autumn on our leisurely rides together. We'd still go round our favourite treks or the ride through the fields, with canters being thrown in when she wanted to. She was such a super fit little horse, and it was always great to finish off our day together, or to start the day off if I had a packed schedule and teaching in the evening.

The decisions for the future were being made between the young ones, breeding, and the horses and ponies. That winter, I decided to downsize the riding school dramatically again, as staffing was a huge issue. It meant I would handle most of the work myself, but would not need to worry about the yard when attending shows, etc. Over the next few months, things got back to a more manageable size again, and it gave me more time to do what I wanted and to spend with Sesky. The winter was long, and she and I spent a lot of time in the indoor school, grateful to have somewhere to ride when it was icy outside. And on a few nice sunny days, we took the opportunity to get out along the trekking routes, which was such a treat.

February is always a month I look forward to each year, as it gets lighter, and spring is on its way. This year was going to be particularly exciting with Sesky's foal due, and June couldn't come around quickly enough.

We decided to sell Misty, who went to a lovely home. And with Mari-Claire on the yard with me now, and less horses and ponies to look after, things were much easier. I tried to throw in extra riding time with Sesky whenever I could, but conscious of not doing too much with her as she was in foal. She liked to be kept ticking over and I knew that, like the last time, she would let me know when the time was right to be finishing up. At that stage, though, she was blooming, looking amazing, and as fit as a fiddle. She looked like she was enjoying being in foal again.

The month of March was when I stopped riding Sesky. I'd changed her girth quite a few times over the previous month or two to keep her comfortable, as she was getting bigger and bigger, but she was still full of energy. Then towards the middle of March, when she was being un-tacked, she looked at me as if to say we were finished. As I patted her tummy, I was thinking the same, so the saddle and bridle now headed off to be cleaned, oiled, and stored away once more.

Over the next few months, I enjoyed seeing Sesky out in the sunshine in the field for a time, and waddling about as she pleased. She would still try and throw in that odd run and buck at the fence if the trekking ponies and I went past, though. And when she wanted in, we knew about it! She would stand at the gate, stretching her head over and patiently waiting, neighing if we came past, and making the odd snatch at the ponies. That was always the best time to bring her in; if we missed the opportunity, she would walk away and not come in for hours, being naughty when we tried to catch her.

It was funny to see how big she was getting as she walked, and on some days I was a bit worried that she might just make it in and out of the stable door entrance and no more!

Chapter 8

Grounded

The next few months were spent pampering Sesky when she was inside. Even in-between my treks or teaching, I would be found in her stable or close by, checking on her. When I was passing by the field where she was wandering about quite happily by herself, I would always give her a quick glance to make sure she was alright.

The end of my working day could not come quickly enough to finish up and spend some time with her, and at the weekends, if we were at a show, I was always keen to get back to check with the staff on the yard how she had been doing during the day.

We'd had a remarkably busy few months with trekking and teaching, and in May I had to make a few visits to the chiropractor, followed by a visit to the hospital for an X-ray for an annoying old back pain that would not go away. It was as a result of landing on my bum in the field, after being bucked off a pony, but I guess you just get up and say 'ouch' and carry on. I probably should have dealt with it years before, but now I had no choice. It meant the inconvenience of having to rest, which was a real nuisance, and was the last thing on my mind!

I reduced the number of treks I did and rode less. And it probably helped with Sesky being in foal, because I didn't mind about not getting in the saddle for a few days here and there. But I certainly had no intention of hanging up my riding gear anytime soon.

Sesky only had a few weeks left until her due date, so I was keeping a close eye on her. She still liked her walk out to the field for an hour or so, but she was often glad to get back in for a rest, as she did not enjoy just standing about for too long. She liked to be on the move – just like me.

The evening checks increased, and later I peeped in through the night, too, as I remembered that there had been no warning signs the last time. Her bed was nicely banked up, thick with golden straw – something I always attended to last thing at night while she stood happily munching her hay. Everyone else hated mucking out this bed when Sesky was out, because it was so thick and every piece of straw that had to be taken out needed replaced. They knew I would be checking if I had not done it myself. It had to be left perfect, as I was so pernickety about that, especially now.

With June firmly under my feet, the end of the month was eagerly awaited; it could not come quickly enough. Sesky was only going out for an hour to loosen off each day, and was soon back at the gate, waiting to come in. She seemed happier in her stable, or liked to stand outside being groomed, with the odd walk to the hosepipe at the back to have her tail washed. Jim had come to remove her shoes and trim her feet once more, but it was difficult for her to stand to have it done. I also liked to pull her mane and tidy it and her tail, knowing it was not a job to be doing when she had a foal jumping about the stable. And there's no doubt Sesky loved the attention and her grooming. I think it probably relaxed her, as she would almost fall asleep as she stood outside in the sun, or in the stable with her head resting over the door.

The large horse first aid box sat outside her stable door, along with everything and anything else I might need when this foal was born. And I had already warned the vet that if anything went wrong, he should expect a phone call round about the 28th of June – even if it was in the middle of the night. He just laughed, because he had dealt with me for years, and knew that if I called it must be urgent.

In the few weeks leading up to her due date, I was not keen to go anywhere off the yard. If I had to walk out with the treks, I would leave the longer ones to the girls and only go on the short half hour trips, where I knew I always had a signal on my mobile phone if needed!

The days and nights came and went, and I felt like a night warden most of the time, desperate not to miss the birth of this foal.

On the 28th, I checked Sesky about 7pm, after I had finished teaching and chatting. Everyone had finished up and had gone home, so the yard was nice and quiet a little earlier than usual. As I looked at her, it occurred to me that she could have the foal that night, so I left her for a while and went back to check her at 8pm.

Until then, I had been expecting that the foal would be born during the night – like the others – but it looked like this one was definitely on its way. Mari-Claire was on her way to collect our dinner, so I quickly phoned her and said she should probably turn back if she wanted to see this foal being born.

I went in to Sesky to give her some gentle pats, but she looked at me helplessly as she paced up and down, so I stepped back for a while to let her get on with what she had to do. By now, the little cats were all starting to gather, with one or two appearing outside Sesky's stable and one up on the wall. It seemed the news was out that this little foal was going to appear.

About 40 minutes later, with a gentle pull from me, a beautiful little foal appeared. As it lay on the straw, an exhausted Sesky whimpered to it, while I released its face into the open air and cleared its airway until its little head started shaking. Relieved, I stood back again and witnessed the motherhood bond beginning. It was beautiful to watch Sesky administer gentle licks while the foal whimpered and jerked around on the straw, and the tears of joy and delight were running down my face. Sesky eventually stood and gently moved her head down towards the foal, licking its face and body as she gave it a few gentle nudges. Then she looked at me and I gave her those familiar 'Good girl, Sesky' pats to congratulate her on a job well done.

After a little while, the little foal scrambled to get up onto its feet, but it kept falling again as its legs just didn't know what to do. Sesky stood by, neighing with encouragement and giving a few gentle nudges as she licked. It made a few attempts to get up, and just when we thought it was going to stand, down it went again, falling forwards. I realised then that it might be a good idea to remove the water bucket, which I had left in due to the earlier excitement. Then I went back to stand in the inside corner of the stable again.

The foal pushed up using all its strength and determination and, with legs like jelly, it wobbled about with its bottom in the air, trying to work out how to get the front end up, too. At last, it managed to stand, whimpering to its mother, as though it was wondering what came next.

The foal edged its head forward to try and suck Sesky's back leg. Then, with a few nibbles towards its back and bottom from Sesky – and a slight guide from us – it latched on to have its first suckle from its mother. What a pleasure to see; Sesky was finally a happy mum again, and she stood contentedly as she allowed the foal to drink.

When the foal dropped back down, after trying a few steps, I got the chance to spray its cord and check what we had – a little filly foal once again! This beautiful little black foal looked stunning, with a larger white star shape on her forehead, a little white mark just below, and a white snip by her nose. A small white blotch on the lower leg was the only other mark she had. She was the cutest little thing ever.

I gave her a little check over as she snuggled up into the straw, then I checked Sesky to make sure everything was all right with her, before tidying up and bringing some fresh straw and clean water back in. Sesky stood proudly over her foal, giving her the odd little lick and nudge, and I left them to it.

All our little cats that had hung around during the evening had now wandered off, as though their job was done, too. It had certainly been an exciting evening, and dinner was extremely late, although no-one seemed to bother. We were all delighted at having this beautiful new addition grace us with her presence, and particularly at a very reasonable hour of the day.

After about an hour or so, I quietly walked back up to check on them from outside the door. The foal was having another drink, which was good, and Sesky put her head up and neighed as if to say to let me know they were fine. Being a lovely summer's night, it was still and quiet for them to have a rest. The yard was quiet, too, as if all the other horses knew it was rest time for everyone. I went back up about midnight, having left a small light on in the shed behind, so that I could check on them without disturbing them too much. Both mum and foal looked settled, sleepy, and content. So I happily turned around and headed to bed, knowing that the all-night watches were, thankfully, over.

A few hours in bed and I was up with the birds, briskly making my way to Sesky's stable first. What a difference a few hours can make. When I got there, the little foal was already darting about the stable, her little black body gleaming like a new diamond, while Sesky was proudly watching her stunning little addition.

I managed to clean out the stable the best I could, with her jumping excitingly around, and put in the fresh straw and water. Sesky was looking forward to her breakfast that morning, so I left them to get to know each other a little more, and to have a nice rest.

Later, while I was giving Sesky a wash over her tail and back legs, and she stood happily munching her fresh hay, the little foal was inquisitive about what I was doing. She would walk over to me and stretch her head out to my bucket, then on hearing the water, she would run in front

Sesky and her foal in the stable that morning.

of Sesky and come round the other side to stand and watch again.

That morning, we decided to name the little foal Tsunami. As she had been bred by the stallion Tornado, we thought it was quite an appropriate name, and it seemed to suit her. My mum was eager, as always, to come and see the new addition, so she arrived with her husband, Alex, before the morning was over. As usual, when she visited, she had brought all her bags of carrots for the horses and ponies, with special treats for Sesky. They were delighted to see Tsunami before anyone else, and we took plenty of happy new family photos.

For the next few days, we enjoyed showing the new foal to everyone, and proud mum Sesky was in the middle of all the celebrations. I had also arranged a quiet weekend for myself, so it was great to spend time with the friendly youngster and to see how adorable she was with Sesky.

The first day of putting them into the field was exciting, and Tsunami had to be coaxed out of the stable, as she did not want to come off the straw onto the concrete ground. Sesky was a little anxious as to what was happening, and could not stand still while she waited on her. With a little persuasion and help, though, we managed to get the foal to spring across the bits of straw on the ground, and immediately Sesky flew to her side to accompany her on the short walk to the field.

When we got there, Sesky ran off into the field, with the little foal galloping frantically behind her to catch up. At that moment, Sesky was only thinking about her bid for freedom and blowing off a bit of steam... until suddenly she realised she had forgotten something, and hastily turned round and made her way to the foal. With some neighing and whimpering, the youngster was given plenty of reassurance, and we could all breathe a sigh of relief as we watched them together again. The weather was perfect for getting them out, and seeing them in the field together was a lovely sight – one I had looked forward to for a long time.

We had great fun days watching them in the field, with the foal keeping everyone amused as she discovered new things. One day, when they had been turned out, Sesky dashed off with the foal running after her, as she often did. This time, though, the youngster jumped into the air and over a bush, to which I excitedly shouted, 'She can jump!' I was laughing, but already I was thinking and hoping we had a little showjumper in the making.

It was an exciting year with Sesky and the foal, and it was always a thrill to jump up out of bed early to visit them first before I fed the yard, then muck them out before my day began properly. The pair were also a great talking point for tourists to the yard and clients, who liked to have a look and find out how they were doing.

I used to love looking over the stable door later when mum and foal had come back in from the field; to see Sesky standing guard, with little Tsunami snuggled up in the straw at the back of the stable, was lovely.

Feeding times were always amusing, as the foal would be trying to get into Sesky's feed bucket to see what she was eating. Sesky, meanwhile, would nudge her away at every attempt, with her head firmly placed in the bucket and the foal left looking under Sesky's neck, just waiting for the first opportunity to see what she had. It was a moment of cuteness I will never forget.

Sesky was a brilliant mum again, and very attentive to the foal, but neither of them minded me being in the stable; they actually enjoyed the attention. The livelier the foal was getting, the harder the mucking out was, particularly on days when they could not go out due to the weather. When the fresh straw was put in, Tsunami always jumped excitedly into it, having a good roll about before the bed could be finished. Sesky watched her jumping about with almost a surprised expression on her face, her ears stretched up, neighing at the foal as she flew around the stable. I'd usually leave them to have their crazy ten minutes of fun, and go off to make up the hay for feeding, then come back and finish off when the foal had settled down. By then, she would be having her drink, and would lie down once again while I fixed the bed round about them. She was certainly a lively little one.

The autumn and winter months seemed to be upon us before we knew it, and the foal was getting bigger and cheekier all the time, with Sesky occasionally having to put her firmly in her place a few times in the stable. The outings to the shows continued, and I got better at leaving the yard, knowing they would be fine until I got back. I was always excited to return and rush to see them, eager to find out what they had been up to during the day and to know that all was well.

When I'd be grooming Sesky, the foal would watch, but she enjoyed the process, too. When it was her turn to be brushed, she would nibble at my legs and arms gently, as though I was Sesky, then run off in the stable once she'd had enough.

Standing daydreaming, I studied Sesky carefully. She looked so white now, having lost the odd bits of grey over the years. I had always taken ages to groom her, as I liked her to look clean with no stains, so maybe it was all that grooming that had made her whiter. At least, that's what my friends used to joke! In contrast, the foal was a glossy, shiny black.

The little one had come up with a new game in the stable. With Sesky's water bucket being quite large, Tsunami would often try and put one leg – or two – into it. When she felt the water splashing on her, she would jump backwards, almost pulling the bucket over, too. Luckily, it was a large, soft plastic one, so usually it would just bend a little and spill some water out. Eventually, I put it inside an old tyre, to stop it moving when she tried to tug at it. I think she did everything to the bucket apart from sit in it… although that almost did happen once or twice.

With the nights getting colder as the winter drew in, and wind and rain blowing from all angles, I decided that Sesky and the foal should move across to the other barn to be under more cover. We had a large stable in there, with a gate to close over the top of the door if needed, so it would be ideal.

Sesky had been in the barn before and would not bother, so I decided to move them before the weather got much worse. One day, they had some time out in the field, and instead of going to their usual stable, they were led into the barn, with the foal following behind. As they were tired from being out in the field, it seemed the best time to move them in. The top gate was closed over for the first night or two, to get the foal used to the different noises from the wind on the high roof of the barn and its new surroundings, then it could be left open again. Thankfully, they enjoyed their change of stable and were quite content.

As we went into the new year, it was time to think about separating Sesky and the foal, who was now seven months old, getting big, looking great, and feeding well. I hated having to separate them and, as before, kept putting it off. But I knew deep down that it had to be done. I left it until the end of January… then decided February would do. With about a month left before we started going back out to the shows, I was keen to see them settled so that I wouldn't worry about them when I was away.

The plan for that day was that they would be out in the field as normal, to take the freshness off them and hopefully tire them out. The stables were prepared, and I was keen for everything to go like clockwork so that there would be as little upset as possible.

Sesky and Tsunami were brought in from the field and their legs hosed off as normal, with a few people on hand to assist. Then they were walked, with Sesky in front and Tsunami behind, into the barn and down to the stable. This time, however, I kept walking Sesky past the stables, up the step to the other entrance of the barn, and quickly across to her original large stable outside. I closed her in as quickly as I could, with her probably just presuming that Tsunami was following behind. Then I ran back across to the other barn where Tsunami had been walked straight into the stable, not realising that the door had been closed quickly behind her, without Sesky being there. Her head-collar was removed and she was given some soothing pats before being left to have a few minutes to settle as normal. She continued to munch her hay, and seemed not to be concerned, as we watched anxiously to see what she would do.

They had previously spent few occasions apart leading up to separation, and everything seemed fine for a short while... and then it happened. Sesky started neighing, as she had now realised Tsunami was not coming, and she got louder and louder from the other barn. Hearing this, Tsunami started pushing to the door, looking to the entrance of the barn, and neighing back. Now wondering what was going on, she started spinning around the stable, running at the door, and looking like she was going to jump out, so we quickly closed over its top gate. She made her annoyance clear when she would lift her front leg up at the gate onto the door, banging it and neighing, then sometimes bucking up at it. But as she would take the odd rest in between tantrums, to nibble her hay or investigate her salt lick, we were fairly sure that she was not yet fully distressed.

As you probably guessed, the famous radio in the barn was turned up to quieten out the neighing noise between them, and we kept an eye on Tsunami as the yard work continued. Everyone was eager to have a peep in at her, as this barn was their favourite one to work in.

To make sure I was still her friend, I went to see Sesky in the other barn, taking half a bucket of carrots and apples with me to soften the blow. She looked at me as though disgusted, but I patted her as she lunged against the stable door with all her strength, neighing furiously, looking across to the other barn. For a while she pounded round that stable, swishing her tail with anger and barging at the door again, looking like she wanted to eat me! When I tried to pat her, she shook her head and marched to the back of the stable again.

Thinking it might be a good idea to go in and give her my peace offering, I opened the door and went in, quickly closing it firmly behind me before she came to the front again. But when I offered her the delicious bucket of treats, she looked at it, looked at me, then knocked it straight out of my hands with her head, barged at the front door again, neighing and pacing round the stable, tramping and smashing the apples and carrots firmly into the straw. I'm sure she was telling me, 'This is what I think of that!'

I just looked at her, gave her a few of my 'Good girl, Sesky' pats, and made a quick exit out the stable, as she marched angrily past me once again. As I looked back, I could see her head disappear down to the straw for a minute or two, probably to investigate her mashed carrots and apples and have a nibble. Then she raised her head, dropping the food out of her mouth, and started neighing and barging at the door again. I was just relieved there were big strong door bolts and kick bolts on, to keep her in. Thankfully, no customers were due to visit for a week or so yet.

I managed to resist the temptation to go back to her, deciding to let her calm down a little. But at teatime she was still not amused, so I kept my visit to her stable short, and made sure the door was firmly closed the whole time to keep her in.

Tsunami was still having tantrums from time to time in her stable, and she made it clear she was not happy with us when we went in to sort her hay and feed. The good old water buckets were tipped and dragged about, while the tyre was dislodged from its place, but I guess it kept her busy. Clearly it was going to be an eventful and noisy night, and it looked like I'd be back on my night warden checks.

Things would get quiet for a while, then the odd neighs from either one would start the other off again, and so it continued until the early hours of the morning when I decided the radio was staying up loud and they were settled enough that I was going to bed for a few hours. Fully clothed, I went to sleep on the couch so I could jump up and get out quickly if necessary. I felt as though I had only closed my eyes for a second, but when I looked at the time, I had slept for about three hours, and it was just after 5am.

Marching quickly up to the yard, the radio was blaring as soon as I opened the door, and I was just thankful that there were no neighbours nearby. All was quiet from Sesky's barn as I sneaked past to check on Tsunami first. Apart from the radio, everything seemed quiet, and I wasn't sure whether to be worried or not. Quickening my steps, I found her lying quite happily in the middle of the stable, head upon her leg, curled up, with the plastic water bucket and tyre lying not far from her. When I was spotted, she got up. And as I went in, with the door and gate pulled behind me, she came over to receive a pat, then walked around the stable happily enough. Then I put in fresh hay, which occupied her until the water was sorted and back in.

When the other horses heard the feed buckets, they started neighing. And as Sesky neighed loudly from the other barn, everything started again. Earplugs were the first thought on my mind, although it was lovely to hear them neighing to each other, knowing they recognised the other. I also now knew that they were not too distressed, just a bit mad. This was clearly shown when Sesky began barging the door and pacing around the stable. It seemed she had stopped for a while during the night, as her large pile of hay had been eaten. And she had devoured her morning breakfast with her warm bran mash added in – something she loved every so often, and which I always gave her after foaling and at times like this. She had a habit of splashing it everywhere when it was eaten, and I always found it amusing to see her messy face afterwards.

The neighing continued for a good week or so, on and off, and to everyone's dismay I kept the radio on loud to distract them. Once they became quieter, the radio was turned down slightly, although it was kept on during the night for a while.

When she was more like herself, Sesky was turned out along with the other horse, Copper. The two had been good friends in the past, and would usually give each other a good 'run for their money', as we would say, when out in the field together. We hoped this would tire Sesky out a bit, so she would be more relaxed when she came in.

Bringing Sesky in at the field gate beside her own and Copper's stable seemed the best option for us, rather than walking down past the other barn where she might hear Tsunami neigh. Something like that had happened with the last foal, and Sesky had run off across to the barn. There was the added advantage that if we caught Copper first and led her across the field, Sesky would run and follow her to the gate, so we could catch her fairly quickly instead of waiting for hours for her to come in.

Some days we would turn Tsunami out in the school for some freedom, and a run and kick about while we watched. Other days, once Sesky had been out and brought back in, Tsunami was led to a small paddock behind the school with one of the small ponies. We had to keep changing which pony went with her, as they soon got fed up with babysitting the crazy youngster! She was always galloping, kicking, and bucking around the paddock as though she would never stop, or might jump out. Then she would have a nibble at the grass and a look at her companion before carrying on again.

The routine seemed to work well over the weeks, and things began to settle down and the radio eventually turned down to normal, although I still left it on at night for 'comfort'. Night checks were eventually back to late on, then all lights off with one more walk up before bed just to listen for any unusual noises or action before turning in myself. Tsunami's top gate was still closed over during the night, but it was being left open for longer periods during the day when we were in the barn to keep an eye on her. Some days she still looked like she would try to jump over the door if the neighing started.

Later, we had to keep the door closed during the day when the field-kept horses and ponies came in and were tied up along the corridor in the barn for lessons or treks. This was just too exciting for Tsunami, and it would look as though she was going to jump out and join them. Putting her little field companions in the corridor in front of her stable, though, helped to calm her down, as they would have the cutest little neigh to each other, and Tsunami would munch her hay, watching what was going on as she calmed back down.

Having a few small and suitable ponies to take turn about in the paddock with her made life easier, and changing them around meant she didn't get too attached to any particular one. There were lots of little things like that which we tried to do to keep the peace and make life easier.

Time marched on, and soon the gate was open, everything was almost back to normal, and the radio was switched off at night. Silence once again. I still continued with my late-night checks, as it was one of my favourite things to do. I loved to make sure that all the horses and ponies were settled, and listen to that amazing nibbling of hay as I walked through the pathways at the stables and barns with a sigh of contentment and satisfaction. Finally, I'd give Sesky that last pat and cuddle round the neck before coming away from the stable, hearing the yawning sounds as they all settled or lay down to sleep... Another day done.

One decision that I had not made lightly was to downsize my school again, and to make some changes with the business and staffing. With a heavy heart, I had to find good new homes for some of the horses and ponies, keeping only the ones which were capable of splitting the workload. I took time to find the right homes for the ones that were leaving, as I wanted to be sure that they would enjoy the comfort and care they had been used to over the years. They still deserved the best.

Unfortunately, one other thing I had noticed was that my niggling lower back pain had been more annoying than before. I kept trying to ignore it and not let it interfere with my day or work with the horses, but it was definitely more noticeable than before.

One day, when I was putting the back door of the lorry up, I suddenly had a painful twinge that made me stop suddenly for a bit, and it was still there when I climbed into the cab. But later, the showjumping took my mind off it as I helped and watched. When I went into the collecting ring to lift the practice jump poles, though, I was aware of the niggle again, so I knew I couldn't keep pushing it to the back of my mind forever.

The months ahead were busy with shows, and spring was in the air. Sesky and Tsunami had settled into their new way of life apart, with neither being out in the fields near each other at any time. Tsunami could stand up for herself, as a few of the ponies found out through time, but she was good to handle and catch, especially from the field – unlike Sesky. She did have a good bit of Sesky's younger nature and character in her, though, and she was really adorable and lovely to look at.

Quite a little character, just like her mum, I used to think, and she reminded of when Sesky was four years old and what she would get up to when I first got her. Sesky's other foal, Star, was now five years old, and after having a break for a while, she was now back in work. She could also be quite naughty at times, and showed some of Sesky's spirited moments. One for the watching, I decided! It was hard to believe how the years had passed with these two youngsters, and Sesky now 16 years old. Time just seemed to gallop by.

A busy season with teaching, trekking, and the shows, kept me on my feet most of the time, and I was aiming to put Sesky back into work for the beginning of the summer. A few rides in the school to introduce her back to work, and some leisurely walks out on our own, was a nice way to bond again. I was keen to ride again, but some days that niggle in my back would remind me it was not going away, no matter how much I tried to ignore it.

The Highland Show was always one to look forward to and marked on the calendar throughout the pony years. As Mari-Claire had qualified again for the show, it was a weekend when we – and a few horses – stayed on the showground. It was busy but really good fun; it also gave us the chance to mingle with friends, and have a look around once the horses were settled after the jumping.

Sesky was staying at home, and having the weekend in and out the field, enjoying the rest between our riding again. But I always liked to phone back to the yard at night to make sure everything was all right before going to bed. We headed back from the show on the night it finished, which gave us time to catch up and clear the horse box the next day, as Mondays were set aside as a day off after a show weekend.

The next fortnight seemed a bit of a struggle for me, and in the middle of July I found myself choosing not to ride Sesky, which was totally unheard of! I didn't want to ride the ponies out on the treks either, and would walk out with them only if I had to, as that back niggle was starting to scream for attention. Cutting out the harder jobs on the yard for a week or two, I thought somehow the 'rest' would help, but this time the pain was not for disappearing and I had to accept defeat when picking up the pony's hoof to clean it out proved to be total agony.

I continued with teaching, trying to put a brave face on, but was well aware that I was choosing the easier options in the classes rather than ones that would involve moving jump stands or poles. I knew I was not my usual self.

Then one morning… it happened. I went to get out of bed, and basically could hardly move due to the agonising pain in my lower back. Eventually, I somehow managed to get ready and got myself to the doctor's for 8am, leaving the morning yard duties to someone else. Heaven knows how I managed, but I just knew I had to get there.

At the doctor's, I chose to sit in the car until it was my turn, wishing that they would hurry up so I could get it over with and back to work. However, I soon learned that it would not be that easy. Instead, I was given strict instructions to get home and not do anything, with a few painkillers thrown in.

With no improvement, I went back the following week, and the doctor made a referral to the hospital for a back scan. When I was told that it could take at least five to six months for an appointment, if not longer, I genuinely thought they must be joking! I could not ride my horse, I could not teach through the pain, and I was totally unable to do any everyday tasks, including housework; it was total nightmare! Luckily, the yard and horses were in good hands, everything was taken care of, and I knew Sesky would be alright.

Mum and Alex would come to visit some days, bringing chocolate and gifts as a pick-me-up, but even that did not help. I was just extremely annoyed with everything. I'd never been one to take any sort of tablet, but now found myself watching the clock to see when I could take my next dose. The pain just seemed to be everywhere, and I was fed up and anxious.

For weeks, I struggled on, waiting for word of the scan, but it felt like a nightmare I could not get out of. Even after several calls and no reply, I was becoming more frustrated, and decided to set up an appointment with my chiropractor in the hope of finding a solution. Finding out that she could not do anything, as the problem seemed serious, was a final blow. I could not face the prospect of waiting months on end to hear from the doctors; the pain was unbearable, and I was so angry, particularly as I was hardly ever ill; even a cold never usually bothered me!

After several more weeks, my sister Edith came to stay to help out, as I could not even stand to make a cup of tea. Even holding the teaspoon was painful, and I was a nightmare to be around. Heaven knows how she, and anyone else, put up with me. I just had to accept defeat and let her take over.

Several more weeks passed and I still heard nothing from the hospital, so I made a call again to the chiropractor. This time, after a lengthy discussion, it was decided that she would make the arrangements for me to go private. The last few months had been a total nightmare, and I just had to get this sorted out.

Within the week, a letter came for my private scan on 10th September at 3pm; I still had heard nothing back from the doctors and the hospital. Using every bit of willpower and strength I possessed, I got taken to the Nuffield Hospital for my scan, then back home, and it wasn't long before I was informed that I would need back surgery, which was pencilled in for the 20th of November, 2002.

The date was clearly marked on the calendar, and I counted down every second. My sister and my family were absolute angels to put up with me, and on many a day I do not know how Edith did not walk out. Mum even dreaded visiting, knowing she couldn't help and that I was unbearable. But she still came. I realised that if I made it to the 20th of November without somebody killing me first, it would be an achievement!

I was admitted to hospital the day before, and informed that I was first in line for the operation at 9.30am the following morning. That was a relief, as I was feeling really anxious and scared. In the morning, I was taken to the operating theatre and clearly remember them saying we would count down from ten… and eight was the last I heard! As you're reading this book, you'll be aware that I did wake up again.

In the recovery room after the operation, for some reason I started sobbing my heart out, and had no idea what had happened to me. But with some reassurance from the nurse beside me, I eventually calmed down. I was then moved into my own room, hooked up to all sorts of machines, and with a nurse at my side while I fell in and out of sleep.

When I finally woke up properly and remembered where I was, I immediately began bombarding the poor nurse with questions, only to be informed that the doctor would be round soon, and I had to stay lying where I was.

When he finally came, he explained that the back surgery had lasted for about eight hours, instead of the three or four which he had originally anticipated. He explained that he'd had to remove bits that had developed round the spine area, which was trickier than expected, and had involved fixing several discs. However, he said, everything looked promising.

Delighted with the news, my first question of course was when I would be able to ride my horse, but he simply replied that they had to get me walking first. I admit I panicked a little at that, and as soon as he left, I tried to get out of bed then vaguely remember nurses coming in...

When I woke, it was the next morning and the nurse offered me a drink and asked if I was going to behave myself today. I had no clue what she meant!

I was told that I would be helped up after lunch that day, so the morning just dragged as I waited anxiously, watching the hands move slowly around the clock. When the time came, I was helped to do a few steps and back again, but I had not realised it would be so difficult, and I was glad to be back in bed. I was helped to try a few more steps again before dinner – a few more than earlier – but it felt soul-destroying that I could not walk normally yet.

The next day, the same happened, and over a few days I made slight improvement. When I eventually walked the length of the corridor, it seemed like such a huge achievement, even though I felt as if I'd run a marathon at the end of it. I had never realised this would be so hard.

With physios on the job, I then had to show I could walk up some stairs before being considered to go home at the end of the week. While she was with me and explaining this, we were attempting to go up four steps, and I was looking at the top step with sheer dread! But by the time the eighth day came, I had done it and was discharged, along with a letter for my doctor to explain about the back surgery and a list of do's and don'ts.

When I got home, there was a letter waiting for me to say that my NHS scan was arranged for the following March. Thank goodness I had eventually decided to go private!

I was determined not to mess up my rehabilitation, so I followed the doctor's instructions and did everything by the book, building up my daily walks, and religiously doing my exercises. Sesky's stable was the first in line to walk to, then each day I would stretch to reaching a few more, until I was finally able to get round the yard. The first time I managed to walk down the long driveway was a huge accomplishment, but then with dread I turned and realised I had to make it all the way back! It was only sheer determination that got me through that day.

The start of December came, and I received my return appointment to see the back surgeon in January. Sesky, having had a few months off while I was grounded, was enjoying her cosied-up life of eating and suitable days in the field. I was making more frequent visits to see her, but nothing else; I was determined to be good and not overdo things.

January arrived slowly, and I was driven to my check-up appointment in plenty of time. I sat nervously in the waiting room, desperately watching the clock once again – it had become a habit of mine over recent months, but I was still no better at it.

When the doctor gave me the all-clear, my first question was when I could drive and ride. The driving I could start slowly and build it up, he said, but unfortunately the riding would have to wait for several months yet – with the word 'several' being exaggerated loudly and firmly.

'What about driving my horsebox?' I asked cheekily.

'Drive your car first and see how you are,' was the reply.

Satisfied with that, and with a big smile on my face, I left before he could say any more.

And drive my car I did… the next day. I made a short trip to the local shop for chocolate, and back. Mission accomplished! I thought I would build on this over the next few weeks, while I continued to build up my walking time. Near the end of the month, I added some light duties about the house, then a little half day or so on the yard messing about, with nothing too strenuous and just the occasional light groom for Sesky. Tsunami just seemed to have grown so big in the time I hadn't seen her, while Star was still being as cheeky as ever.

I was starting to feel a bit more normal again and was happy with the driving and walking, but I was seriously starting to eye up that horsebox. February was always a month to get back out to shows after the winter, if the weather was good, so I did not want to miss out. And after all, I felt fine. I was desperate to watch Mari-Claire compete again with the horses, and to take them there myself, rather than relying on someone else.

The temptation could not be put off any longer. With a passenger on board, that afternoon I finally decided I was taking the horsebox for a run to the next village and back. Bursting with excitement, I went carefully down the long drive, telling myself, *What harm could a few miles do?*

When we returned, I parked up with sheer delight on my face and not a twinge in my back anywhere. Driving my horsebox again had been easier than driving my car, and I was optimistic that we could consider heading off to the shows the following weekend. The doctor had not stipulated how long I needed to drive for before attempting the horsebox, and I felt absolutely fine now! Thinking back to those first days after the operation, I would never have imagined then that I would be back driving the horsebox again in a few months. But willpower and determination had brought me back to good health.

February came and went, and my few check-up visits to the chiropractor went well, which allowed me to carry on with life without thinking about my back again – except for riding. Even though several months had passed and I was so desperate to ride Sesky again, I was a bit anxious about getting on her and something happening, so it was a chance I was not yet willing to take. I would not even sit on one of the ponies in case I fell off, so I guess I knew inside that I was not ready.

While I was still building up my own strength, I came up with the idea that Sesky could go back into foal. And as she had been out of work for quite some time during my absence, I would not need to worry about getting her ready again. It would also give me something to look forward to, and keep my mind off the riding. *In fact,* I wondered, *why not have two foals?*

Copper, the other jumping horse, had been forced to retire due to arthritis in her hocks, so she and Sesky could each have a foal at the same time. It would be good for Copper, as she was fit and well enough, and not in any pain with the arthritis; she just could not jump and was not too pleased at being ridden, so her retirement days had come early.

With two foals now on the wish list, the plan of action was made, and stallions chosen. After a couple of unsuccessful attempts to get them into foal, I decided I wanted them to have one more try. The timing had to be perfect before it was too late.

Scans had to be carried out for checks on both horses, weeks apart on both occasions. Each time, this involved the semen being ordered again, me being at the airport twice for collection as soon as it arrived, and having staff and the vet – already warned of the estimated time of arrival – waiting with the horse tied up in the corridor, for me to return. I watched closely, willing it to be successful; the atmosphere was a bit tense. Thankfully, though, job complete, all we had to do now was hope and wait again. I was a little concerned that with Sesky now being 17 years old, it might just be a bit too late for her, while Copper – though a bit younger – had not had a foal before. Only time would tell.

Awaiting the next scan, I was trying not to build up my hopes too much, but in October 2003 my prayers were answered, and they were both in foal! I could not wait to tell everyone and anyone that we were going to be having two foals this time. Being good friends in the field before,

Sesky and Copper would now have field days together as expectant mums until the following June/August, as they were due within weeks of each other. Having two foals at the same time was going to be exciting, and I could not wait.

For months I'd had to keep myself occupied without riding, but I was now getting the urge to try. Still a little anxious, I decided one day to have a shot on one of the school's ponies, which at least got me back into the saddle for a bit. Attending the shows and watching the horses compete took up a lot of my time, so there was less time and temptation for me to overdo the riding. Being fully back into my teaching and training, I threw myself back into work and organising my lessons again, planning the training for the winter and spring for the junior riders in the school.

I guess sometimes in life we tend to forget what the 'simple, normal, everyday' things are, as we plough on and never take time to think. And I was surprised to realise in 2004 that I was then in my tenth year of having my riding school and trekking centre. How time flies!

The winter and a new year always seemed to be a time for making new decisions and planning for the year ahead, and that year was no different. I decided that Star, Sesky's foal, was going to be moved on. Now over six years old, she was still quite a handful to ride and could be quite naughty at times, so it was the best option.

As spring arrived, so did the temptation to ride again. The school pony was tacked up, and soon I was trotting round with the odd canter thrown in. I was ready to ride my treks out once more.

Seeing Sesky and Copper grow together through their pregnancy was lovely. Watching them roam and play about in the field, I just could not wait for the foals to arrive. The eleven months of pregnancy seemed so long, and although Sesky had experienced no problems with her previous pregnancies, I hoped Copper would be the same. Sometimes I worried in case things would go wrong, and wondered if it would be double the trouble, or double delight!

With both being due within weeks of each other, the night checks began again. Sesky had previously given birth on her date or thereabouts, but this was Copper's first, so I wanted to be ready in case she went early. And what if they both went on the same night, and I had no-one on hand to help? Or if I was with one and missed the other? I was getting into panic mode! I had started to keep a detailed notebook, marking down any changes with either of them. This was kept in their first aid box outside their doors, to be checked every time I came back from being off the yard.

With four weeks to go to the first expected date, I was going nowhere. Their stables were near each other, which made life much easier for the usual jobs and day and night checks. It meant I could nip from one to the other, especially in between teaching my lessons. The young riders attending their training days enjoyed being given the full run down of Sesky and Copper, watching them change throughout the eleven months as they awaited their foals. Although I did leave out the part about how they got that way; that was for their parents to explain!

Keeping myself busy with the lessons and treks was a good way to pass the time, and although I enjoyed riding the ponies, I couldn't help but compare the experience to riding Sesky. And as soon as a lesson or trek was over, I was eager to get back to the stables as excitement rose.

Chapter 9

Offspring

O ne summer's night – well, really the early hours of
the morning – Copper surprised us by deciding to
have her foal weeks early. I had known she was due first,
but hadn't expected her to go that early. So it was a shock
when I went to do my night checks and found this little
foal lying on its own at one side of the stable, with Copper
looking terrified at the opposite side. I quickly reassured
her that everything was alright – well, I hoped it was – then
had to run to the house to get help, as I had no mobile
phone signal.

Copper didn't seem to want to know, and just looked at
us helplessly as if to say, 'Where did that come from?' The
little foal lay hardly moving, and we knew it needed its
mum, but Copper was jumping round the stable, trying to
stay as far away from it as possible. I'd never experienced
this with Sesky, and my stomach sank.

I had a bottle and milk substance from the vet on hand
if needed, but that was the last thing I wanted to do. I
hoped that the bonding between mother and foal just

needed a little assistance from us. Getting Copper's head collar on, we had to try and introduce her to the foal.

The cats, as normal, were all around the stable and on the wall, wondering what was going on, but Copper was having nothing to do with this little foal. Warming it a bit with the straw, I let them both have a brief rest, and then the foal tried to get up. As it did, Copper started spinning round, dragging me with her as she moved away from the foal, snorting, and looking terrified. With Copper being made to stand, the foal again tried to get up on its wobbly little legs. After a few attempts, and collapses, it finally managed to stand wobbling on the spot and, with a little help from us, was guided to its mother. We held Copper firmly as the foal tried to rub onto her, smelling her for probably the first time.

Copper's eyes were almost popping out as she stared at the foal, but after a few exhausting attempts, we got them both together. Copper was still a bit jumpy, but we eventually managed to get the foal towards her enough, and for her to stand and allow it to drink. There were a few kicks at the wall and yelps from Copper, as her little foal got its much-needed drink, but when we were sure we could allow them to stand on their own, we moved back and watched the bond between mum and foal finally begin.

Copper made a few funny noises as she investigated this strange little new arrival, giving it a few licks and nudges as she settled down. But she looked much happier than she had earlier, and we could finally relax and breathe as we watched the little foal take a drink and then flop down, exhausted, on the straw.

Once things had settled a little, we had the chance to check the foal over, and could see we had a little colt chestnut foal, much to the delight of Mari-Claire. He had beautiful golden chestnut colouring over his body and legs – different to Copper's liver chestnut colour – and the same little white star on his forehead as his mum.

After a tiring night, our job was done, and we left them to have a bonding session. I popped in for a quick check on Sesky, who was stretching out over the door, eagerly wanting to see what was going on. I gave her a comforting pat to say she would be next, then headed off to bed, while the cats disappeared once again into the darkness of the night.

The morning light saw me springing out of bed and eagerly running up to the stable to check everything. By the time I looked over the door, both Copper and the foal were happily standing, with the foal drinking contentedly. After a quick run three doors along to check Sesky, stable feeds in, duties done, I went back to check the little foal out again. He was adorable and so friendly, while Copper stood nearby, carefully watching. She was now looking like a protective and loving mum, and she gave him some soft neighs to come close as she stepped towards him.

I made a happy phone call to the vet that morning to say the first arrival was here, earlier than expected, and explained that things had been a bit of touch and go at the start, so he made a visit that morning to check them out. After giving them both a jag, he announced that he was satisfied with them both and that there was nothing to worry about. 'One down, one to go,' he said, as he climbed back into the car, and my heart jumped at the thought of it.

That morning, after some discussion, we decided to name the foal Chester, and we could now look forward to Sesky's arrival.

Copper was the complete opposite to Sesky. As she was turned out into the field for the first time with the foal, she made sure she was not going too far from its side. Making sure he was right beside her coming out of the stable door, it seemed he did not need much encouragement and almost skipped behind her up the drive to the field. Entering the field, Copper turned to make sure he was right at her side, then slowly trotted off, checking he was close by. It was lovely to see him springing in the air, finding his new freedom space without wandering too far from his mother.

Sesky had been constantly watched before, but even more so now with Chester arriving early. So, my nightly checks consisted of Sesky, then Copper and the foal, then Sesky again, just to make sure nothing had changed while I was out.

Her due date grew ever closer, until one afternoon, when the yard was much quieter with lessons and I had some time before my next one, I popped in to see Sesky and found her pawing the ground and pacing about the stable. She was in labour!

I ran to the other barn quickly to tell them the news, and the yard now was on red alert. Determined not to move from outside that door, I watched eagerly, camera ready to ensure I didn't miss anything. I duly shouted across the yard, 'If Sesky does not have this before my lessons, you will need to do them!' I was going nowhere.

With a few days to her due date, it seemed Sesky was having her foal early, too. Must be the summer air! As Sesky neighed to me, I went inside just to let her know I was there, but let her carry on. After a while, she looked slightly more distressed than she had before, as she lay on the straw and attempted to deliver the foal. I could see that she was struggling to get the shoulders out, so decided a little pull from me might help.

Within minutes, the little foal appeared. I cleared its face and its little mouth, and watched it give a few splutters and a shake of the head, then I stood back and watched. Sesky turned on the straw to be closer to it, then she licked it with a little whimper as it lay on the blanket of birth. Within no time it was lying with its legs sprawled out and head eventually up, while Sesky licked it so gently. It was just beautiful to watch.

Sesky with Adonis just after he was born

The little foal was once again jet black, and as it wriggled about, we could see it had three white socks on the legs, and a little white blaze stripe mark down the middle of his face, running from the top of his head to the bottom. They lay there together for a while, quite comfortable and relaxed.

Sesky seemed quite exhausted and sweaty, and she looked like grey silver rather than white as she sat there on the straw. With all eyes eagerly watching, the pair enjoyed their first moments together, and it seemed ages before either of them made a move to get up.

The foal was the first to try. Its legs just seemed to spread out everywhere as it attempted to stand, then down it plumped to the ground. Sesky then got to her feet as she watched and encouraged it to get up again. Several times the foal just about stood, then its legs gave way again. Finally, with gentle licks and nudges from Sesky, and a bit of a rest in between, the foal tried again and wobbled from side to side then managed to make its way to Sesky and balanced onto her. A few nudges encouraged it to go in the correct direction, then it was drinking from Sesky while the proud mother stood quite happily sniffing it. To our delight, we had our second little black colt. It must have been the boys' season!

With all being well, mum and foal checked and settled, the stable door was barricaded off to make sure no-one disturbed them, and I went off – reluctantly – to give the second lesson of the evening. As I walked away, I took time to tell Copper and Chester that his new playmate had arrived!

The lessons could not finish quickly enough that evening as I was desperate to get back to Sesky and the foal. When everyone had gone, I gave Sesky some of her 'good girl' pats to congratulate her on a job well done, then I sat in the corner on the straw just watching them both, and thinking how wonderful it was to see her with her foal again – her third one now with me.

With the relief – and satisfaction – of knowing that both Copper and Sesky had now safely delivered their foals, I could go off and enjoy my dinner, then return to check them all later and look forward to a good night's sleep.

The next morning, I had double the reason to be up with the birds and out. I raced to Sesky's stable first, then back to Copper's, happy that both mothers and their foals were looking great and content. What more could I ask for? Having the day off the yard jobs and no teaching was an even greater bonus, as I could spend the day babysitting from stable to stable, and admiring the new additions.

The next task was to give Sesky's little foal a name. As he'd been off the lovely stallion Padinus (from team Nijhof), who was selected especially for his nature and jumping breeding, we decided that the little foal should be called Adonis. Coming from the Greek name, and meaning extremely good looking and handsome, this suited him perfectly. He was absolutely stunning in all ways, and special – as was Sesky.

The two little foals now had their own identities and natures, and I was pretty sure they would soon become friends.

Copper was used to going out into the field with Chester now, and it was lovely to see them running off with the little foal following behind, having the odd buck in the air. Copper would occasionally gallop round the field while Chester tried to catch up. It was lovely to see them both so happy and Copper enjoying her motherly role after such a rocky start.

Sesky was always looking over from the stable with that neigh of admiration as she watched them run and stroll about in the field, probably wondering when she would get out.

One afternoon, once Copper and Chester had just come back in from the field nice and tired, I decided that it would be a good time to put Sesky and Adonis out. Sesky seemed more than eager to get out of the stable once the head collar was on, and as soon as the door was opened, she marched out, knowing where she was going. Adonis leapt out of the stable behind her. Not bothering about Copper neighing loudly after them, there was only one thing on Sesky's mind, and she made her usual gallop off to freedom, bucking and kicking in the air. This time, though, little Adonis was racing behind, trying not to let her get too far from his sight. His little legs came up to his chest as he darted about the field, shouting after his mum to remember him.

Sesky eventually stopped to look at him, then galloped off again before he could get too close. Finally, she settled at the fence side near the stables, neighing back to Copper, as Adonis caught up with her. It seemed as though she had blown the cobwebs off for a while, as they settled down, with Sesky having a firm roll in the grass to cool off, then jumping back up and shaking her entire body off. Adonis eagerly watched to see what she might do next. Content, Sesky nibbled the grass while Adonis enjoyed a much-deserved drink, and everything settled back down once more. I think they were both ready for their comfy stable bed that night.

For the next few days, we let them out together again, to allow Sesky to blow off steam and for Adonis to settle into his new surroundings. Then it was time to try them all out together.

Although I was desperate to do this, I was still a little hesitant. While they'd had a sniff at each other over their stable doors while the other was being led past, this was going to be completely different. I decided that as Copper was a bit more level-headed and calmer than Sesky, she

Sesky with Adonis in the field.

and Chester would go out into the field first, rather than try to fight their way past Sesky. Then, after they'd had their little trot about and settled down, Sesky and Adonis would follow them out. Seemed straightforward enough... but Sesky had other ideas!

Once out of her stable, the prancing and neighing started, and when she saw the others in the field, she could not wait to get in that gate. She was using all her strength to get there as quickly as possible, while Adonis was jumping all around, wondering what all the fuss was about. He was soon to find out.

Sesky's constant frantic neighing had Copper running up and down the fence excitedly, with Chester close behind. So, someone had to jump the fence and hold Copper back and out of the way, while Sesky and Adonis were led in.

There was a quick push by Copper as Sesky headed to check out Chester and firmly give him a nudge or two, with Adonis tagging on behind. But after that brief moment of disapproval, they were all soon running and galloping across the field, with Sesky and Copper throwing heads at each other, taking off in the opposite directions with the foals racing on. They'd stop suddenly with their tails in the air, and snorting loudly as they looked at each other, then race towards one another once more, with Chester and Adonis trying to catch up. What have we let ourselves in for? I thought. Maybe this was not a good idea!

Giving them time, eventually Sesky and Copper came together, tails still high as they checked each other out, Chester and Adonis prancing around with their tails in the air, too. Then as Copper went towards Adonis, Sesky spun around and kicked out with her disapproval, which chased Copper off. Thankfully, Chester choosing to be beside Copper put an end to that disaster for a while.

As the foals both had a drink from their mums, exhausted with all the effort, they settled and had a lie down, with Sesky and Copper standing guard as they nibbled the grass round about them. We could all breathe again and relax as they happily grazed with their foals nearby.

We watched for a while as they strolled about the field, Sesky and Copper's noses barely touching as they stopped to face each other, then they would nibble the same patch of grass while the young ones stood side by side. The foals took a little time to investigate each other, with a few hesitant steps towards one another and a run back to their mums, then stretching their necks out to investigate a little bit more and a few closer steps. Finally, they got close and had a few playful moments of head nudging and nibbling, before running back to their mums again for security. As the day carried on, they got that bit braver and came beside each other for a time, then whimpered and ran back to their mums again. It was a good sunny day, and eventually they all came in from the field quite tired and relaxed. Copper and Chester were taken to their stables first, then Sesky and Adonis quite happily came in after them. It looked like our new little routine was being set.

As the days and weeks went on, the field days were always amusing. The two youngsters soon became great buddies and liked to investigate everything and anything, with their mums keeping them in their place when they got a bit out of hand.

Having two young colts was different to having the filly foals. Although I had not had two together before, they were certainly more boisterous, I felt, and a bit cheekier. They seemed to develop in character quicker, and were a bit more demanding of their mums in the stable and in the field. Neither was shy to stamp their foot onto the ground to show disapproval if they were not allowed to get too close or have a drink from time to time. A few times they would throw their heads down, bucking and kicking out at their mums on the spot, before running around. As they got older, too, I noticed that the colts would wander off in the field to a good distance from their mums, and ignore the first few calls from either Sesky or Copper before running back. Many a time, after calling and lifting her head with no response, Sesky would run over and give Adonis a nudge, as if to tell him off.

Mucking and skipping out the stable was much harder with the colts being so naughty and lively. You always had to have eyes in the back of your head, as they were so inquisitive and keen to see what was happening, or were trying to knock the wheelbarrow or bucket over. Both were so eager at feed times that they would push into the feed bucket to see if Sesky and Copper were having something they were not. Having hay nets was not a good idea, for the two inquisitive colts. They were delighted at the large pile of hay being placed on the floor. They would often just plump themselves right down on top of the pile to sleep when Sesky or Copper were eating, as if to say, 'You cannot ignore me now,' while the mums just nibbled round about them. I laughed so many times at their antics in and out of the stable. And even just looking at them over the stable doors on the late-night checks, seeing them snuggled up together with their mums, brought a huge smile to my face. Every day was a learning day with these two colts.

I was always eager to show off 'double the trouble', as I called them. And when I was off the yard, I was desperate to get back and find out what the pair had got up to. Copper was a super mum, and I think she enjoyed her new role. It was a new adventure and a life-changing experience for her. Maybe we had found a new job for her in retirement?

Sesky and Copper seemed to stroll about together in the field, and so did Chester and Adonis. There was not too much of a difference in height between them, but I think Chester showed he was the boss at times, and Adonis would go to Sesky for reassurance. Chester was still that lovely golden chestnut, but while Adonis had been jet black on being born, his coat was beginning to go lighter much earlier than Sesky's other two foals had. Was he about to change?

With the winter approaching and the fields getting wetter, the colts would jump about in the muddy parts together, getting into some mess when they rolled about. When grooming them, you were always sure to get a few sore nibbles from these two youngsters, and sometimes the odd kick or barge. When told off, they would just buck and run around the stable, hiding beside their mum – and sometimes kicking her, too. There was never a dull moment with these two, and they always made me laugh.

Time just seemed to go so quickly, and the decision had to be made about when to separate these boisterous young-sters from their mothers. Adonis had a habit of jumping up onto Sesky all the time and being quite cheeky, and you could see she had had about enough of him and was eager to blast away if they were out in the field or in the school for free time. Chester was similar in nature, but not just quite as lively.

I thought back to the time when Sesky had her first foal, Star, with us in 1997. Eight years had passed so quickly, and here I was thinking of separating her from her third foal now. I guess we all just get wrapped up in life and carry on, while time and years just disappear from under-neath us and circumstances change.

This time, since I had two youngsters to separate, I had come up with an idea. With the double upset and constant neighing being double trouble this time, and not knowing how first-time mum Copper would react – or indeed the two lively colts – I decided to send Sesky and Copper to a livery yard not far from me. That way, I could nip along to see them when I wanted.

Adonis and Chester could go into the large indoor stable with the top gate on the door, as it was always used to separate the youngsters. It was big enough, and it meant they could keep each other company. Adonis and Chester had got used to spending some time together running around in the indoor school while their mums had chill-out time in their stables, so it should work.

Everything was arranged, and the plan put into place for the beginning of February. Having a practice run one day, the colts were brought into the large indoor stable from the field, and stood together in there while Sesky and Copper went to their own stables. Everything went well, so the next day we would do it again, and separate them for good. We'd also had a few practices on and off the lorry with the foals, so it shouldn't seem strange to bring it around and use it.

The lorry was parked along the long side of the barn, down from the field gate as normal, then Sesky and Copper were bought in from the field and led down the side in the usual way. However, this time they went straight onto the horsebox one after the other, with the back door quickly closed before they knew it.

Adonis and Chester were led into the indoor stable, and we watched as they investigated everything, then had a nibble of their hay. Happy that it had all gone like clock-work, I drove the horsebox away, with a few odd kicks and bangs coming from the back and some loud neighing as I drove down the drive. I parked the lorry up close to the livery stables then, with some help, the two fiery horses were unloaded, jumping off the ramp, spinning around and neighing as they were led into their new stables. They were put beside each other in a byre part of the yard, which would be their new home for the next few weeks. Sesky was quite angry, pounding round the stable, neighing and barging the door, with Copper looking on then doing the same. Noisy days and nights to follow, I thought. But at least it had a slide-over doorway at the byre to keep them both in, if needed!

Once they were settled as much as possible, I left them to investigate their new surroundings, and drove back. I was eager – but anxious – to see what Adonis and Chester were getting up to. When I ran into the barn to see the girls standing with the top gate closed, I did not know what to expect. But the pair were standing on the trampled-in hay, with some hanging out of their mouths, not a bit of sweat on them or a care in the world. After a bit of fretting in the stable, a few bangs and runs into the door, the top gate had been closed over to stop them hurting themselves, and they had seemed to calm down again. Nothing compared to their mothers! With a sigh of relief, I could relax now, knowing all was well.

They both seemed quite settled for the rest of the day, although feed times were quite amusing with their neighing, as they heard the other horses shout for their feeds on the sound of the buckets. Were they looking for Sesky and Copper, or just their feeds? Both had their buckets placed at either end of the stable. But not being happy with their own, they would try and steal a different bucket, with a few bucks and kicks thrown in – nothing too serious – before returning to theirs. The evening brought some loud neighing sessions and some ramming at the top gate, followed by silence again for a while.

As they settled for the night, the radio was left on for a bit of comfort and distraction. Looking at their bed, there was no point in touching it until the morning. Apart from some fresh straw being put on top, and a big pile of fresh hay, it could wait until morning to be cleared out. The late-night check saw them settled down beside each other, with silence once again.

Early next morning, as normal I was up bright and early and up to the yard, finding them both neighing at the gate and walking around the stable. It was good to see they had eaten a good bit of hay and had been lying on it, and I was delighted to see the water was nearly empty and not spilt, so they had been drinking.

They were excited to get their feed buckets in, kicking them about and nudging each other away as they munched into the feed, then trampling the rubber buckets into the ground as they played with them. I could have stood and watched them all day long.

Later that morning, they spent a bit of time having a run about in the school to burn off some energy, keeping them out of the way while the girls cleared out the trampled and messy bed. What a job that stable was. It proved to be the one that everybody disliked doing, including me!

A trip up to visit Sesky and Copper was next on the day's jobs, and they were still being quite vocal at times, so I was not surprised to be told it had been quite a noisy night. Neither of them finished their feed that morning, nor were they interested in me. I was in the bad books once again.

Their beds had already been mucked out, which showed at least that the staff had been able to get in with them. I was told they were not too bad, 'as long as the door was shut'. And they had eaten a bit from the day before.

While I stood chatting, they settled down, although from time to time made themselves heard loudly as they leaned over their doors neighing. With my special instructions given, I quite happily left them to go back to the yard, and would pop back at night.

Over the next few days, they did get better and settled down, so I cut my visits down to once a day, really just to see them and give them the good girl pats and some treats.

In the meantime, Adonis and Chester kept us all amused, and got really excited when all the other horses and ponies moved about the barn. Thank goodness for the top gate on that stable door at times! They looked adorable together, with Chester still looking golden chestnut, and Adonis having become a much lighter grey all over his body and most of his legs, apart from his white socks. His dark grey neck and face still made the white blaze down his face stand out as before, and he had kept his black mane and tail.

Once everyone had settled down over the next few weeks, I decided it was time to bring Sesky and Copper home. Adonis and Chester were put out in the field to run off some steam for an hour or two and tire them out, and once they were happily back in, I collected the other two. When we returned, Sesky and Copper ran down the ramp, neighing to let everyone know they were back, then jogged to their stables and neighed loudly over their doors. When a few neighs were heard coming from the other barn, Sesky and Copper – standing as tall as giraffes at their doors, ears pricked straight up, and hay hanging out of their mouths – looked over in the direction of the sound. As we all waited for that neighing to come again, everything was quiet.

Sesky and Copper spent a lot of time at the door that day and night, looking over while they ate. Every step of mine was watched as I walked back and forward to the other barn. Their ears were up and eyes peeled, probably wondering where Adonis and Chester were.

The five o'clock feeds provided the answer. As soon as the horses started neighing, the different sounds from Adonis and Chester could be heard, and Sesky and Copper stood at their doors once again like giraffes, neighing frantically back. Luckily enough, the other horses were neighing louder when the feed buckets came out, and Adonis and Chester were soon distracted by their food.

We had a few moments like these over the next week or two. But Sesky and Copper had days out in the fields to run off some steam and tire themselves out, even if the weather was not so good, and it kept them occupied and away from thinking about anything. Soon they were back to their normal selves.

With spring in the air, I had another job on my hands. Having put Adonis and Chester together in the stable to make it easier for the separation from their mums, I now had to think about separating them before they got too attached to each other. While it had helped them settle away from their mums, I didn't know how they would react from being separated from each other.

As they were good at handling, it was decided one day we would just lead them in from the small paddock, hose their feet off as normal, and walk them into the barn. But this time, Adonis would go into their stable while Chester would go into the one next door. Surprisingly enough, it went without a hiccup. With a few neighs over the door to each other, and a bit of neck stretching trying to get nose-to-nose, everything settled down after a few spins about the stable and pushes into the door. They seemed content that they were almost in touching distance from one another, and soon settled down nicely.

Sesky's second youngster Tsunami had been doing a bit of loose jumping over the winter months. She had attended the loose jumping assessments, and was then sent away to be backed and broken, with the aim of following a showjumping career. We thought it was a good option to send her away to have this done professionally, as they would give one hundred percent commitment to the work needing done to help her get a good start to her career. She had matured into a lovely four-year-old, and although a bit grumpy at times in the stable, she was lovely to handle and had always enjoyed her bit of work. Just like Sesky, we could look forward to a future with her.

The discussions now were around another foal, and if I was going to do it, I knew I should do it early this time in case things did not go to plan at the start, as before. The question now was whether to do one, or both together again. Taking into consideration that Sesky was 19 (it was now 2005), time was marching on, but her health and condition were super, and she'd had no problems in the past or with Adonis, so the vet said he could not see any reason why not. Copper, being younger, should be fine, too.

So, two foals were planned again. As we'd talked about using jumping stallions if the time came again, we knew who we had chosen. The process started again, and without wasting any time, Sesky was scanned to make sure she would not be missed. And with Copper already having her stallion chosen, she was off the yard for a bit.

The few months passed, and Sesky had several attempts at getting her into foal. With sweat dripping off her on her last scan and getting quite worked up, it was just not to be this time, and I made the decision then not to try again as I did not like to see her this way. She had given me three of the most beautiful little foals I could ever have wished for over the years, and she had been a proud and smashing mum, so I had no complaints.

Copper did scan in foal that June, and was due the following spring, so we still had another foal to look forward to.

Chapter 10

Willpower

With Sesky now being off the motherhood role, I decided to give her a few weeks of rest again, in and out of the field, then I would bring her back into work. I had ridden a lot over the last month or two and felt confident in riding the school ponies for trekking, so I reckoned I was ready to get back into the saddle with Sesky. I had longed to do it for ages, and just hoped there would be no stopping us now.

Sesky's saddle and bridle were super clean now, and I had a riding plan put together for her in my head. The next shoeing date was changed to getting all four shoes back on this time, and over those next few weeks her mane and tail were tidied and given a good spruce up. I gave her an odd day or two of wild lunging, as it turned out to be, to introduce her back into the working idea, then a few more quieter lunge days, and it showed she was enjoying herself once again. I just had to make the decision now to get on.

After a busy weekend at the showjumping, driving back and forward, I had decided Sesky would spend the day in the field on the Sunday – hopefully to tire her out –

and I would get on her on the Monday. As it was my day off, it meant I would not need to rush anything.

That morning, my thoughts of getting on her after breakfast then dragged out to doing it after lunch – and an extended lunch at that. My saddle and bridle were put outside the door on the stand while I slowly groomed Sesky… and then groomed her once more. I think I was delaying the inevitable, and wondering whether I would be alright on her. When I heard talk outside the stable about how the horse feed had to be picked up, I shouted that I would go for it – only to be firmly told to get on Sesky!

As the car drove away, I knew I had to get on with it. I had chosen the smaller outdoor arena to ride in, just in case anything happened. *But why was I thinking like that? I had ridden Sesky for years, and knew her inside out!* But I guess that back operation must have been playing on my mind. After wasting more time, I got the mounting block in and someone to hold Sesky while I mounted, then I was finally in the saddle!

The yard was quiet that day, so there was nothing to distract her. As we walked around the arena, I heard a voice shouting, 'How long have you been on?'

'Ages,' I replied with a grin, and the girl who helped me walked past with her wheelbarrow, laughing at my little white lie.

Finally, Sesky and I were back together. After a long walk, I decided I'd try a few trots, and we went together like we had never been apart. The canter, though, could wait for another day.

The dismount was not quite as smooth, as I could not believe how wobbly my legs felt. It was certainly enough effort for one day. Tomorrow I'd be up bright and early for my ride, I decided. Then I led Sesky back to the stable with a pat and a heartfelt 'Good girl, Sesky'.

It felt as if we had never stopped for such a long time, but I made the choice to ride the school ponies out on treks until I was fully back into work with Sesky. I wanted to accomplish cantering first, knowing that if she galloped off in the field or trekking path, I would be once again in control of her and well seated. She might be 19 now, but she could act like a fresh four-year-old when she pleased.

Being back on Sesky again felt so good, and it was hard to believe how many years had passed since she'd arrived, and all the things we had experienced together. I'd often reflect on those years when I walked around at night to check all the youngsters, horses, and ponies, then stand and pat her before bed. Over the years we had lost a few horses and ponies through old age, but it's something you try not to think about often, and just put it to the back of your mind and carry on. I suppose we all do the same thing with worries of any kind – just close them off, leave them undisturbed, and hope they might just go away.

It worked for me; I did not like to dwell on things, but just to move on and keep myself busy. Always having something to do was the way I liked life, as I hated sitting about and wasting time. I loved to be thinking about my next day, or even my next goal. And organising my teaching and treks was exciting, and fun, and busy, and I never knew what lay ahead. Family life just seemed to pass by, with everyone getting on with their own hopes and dreams, and making their own way in life.

Sesky getting back into work was my dream again, and she was loving every minute of it as before. She joined me on some of the treks before that winter, with her having her full clip as normal to keep her looking good. We were also back to riding around our own routes again on our 'special together time', enjoying the peace and tranquillity of the countryside on our chosen days or evenings before the wintry days and nights set in. There was never a doubt in my mind now about riding again.

Driving back and forward to the showjumping competitions was hard. Sometimes I did double trips with a changeover of the three horses on board, or Mari-Claire had to choose which ones would go for the day on longer journeys, then later wish we had taken the other ones instead. So, the following spring, after much moaning and grumbling but with the thought of a larger lorry in mind, I decided I would give myself a challenge and try and pass my HGV test. It was something I'd never imagined being able to do, but I was willing to give it a go. After all, what could go wrong? Other than fail it, of course!

My HGV theory book was bought, and I felt I was back to what I used to do with my dressage test sheets. Every place and minute, I had this book balanced somewhere to read and study for my theory test. As I sat waiting on my next client coming in for lessons, it was pulled out of the drawer and almost glued to my face. It ended up under my pillow at night before I fell asleep, after hours of reading repeatedly. And at the horse shows, I sat in the lorry to study in between the horses competing in their classes. There were plenty of amused comments, but I was determined I would do it, no matter how long it took.

When Copper's foal was due, I often placed my chair on the yard outside her stable for hours, as I checked her and studied the book. It was the perfect excuse not to do the normal yard duties and not move from the stable!

It wasn't long until my studies were interrupted by the arrival of the little foal, and all my attention was on the stable once again. In the beautiful springtime weather, we were blessed with the arrival of another little filly foal, shining golden chestnut in colour, with a lovely – slightly bigger – white star again, just like Copper's marking. Proudly attending to her foal from the off, Copper took to motherhood no problem this time.

Sesky, though, showed the grumpy side of nature as she snatched round the door at them as she looked out, biting the stable door, or making the odd pull towards their stable as she walked out to the field, showing her disapproval of them. A little bit of jealousy maybe?

With the HGV theory being stamped into my head, the weeks were flying past, now all I had to do was arrange the test. Pat, who had her own training lorries, organised it for me, and I was soon sitting at the desk in the test room, scared stiff at having to do it on computer – not my speciality. With everything blocked out and my mind staying focused, I got through the test within the allotted time, and blew it apart with a high 90 pass! I was so thrilled; I could have run a marathon without a second thought! Before the outside door could even close, I was straight on the phone to Pat, and my full week's driving course was booked for two weeks' time. The final test would be on the Saturday morning, when the week of training was complete.

When the training week came around, I found it both difficult and stressful, particularly having someone else in the cab. Splitting the driving hours, we were both under a lot of pressure, especially having to learn the split gear box, and I was shattered at the end of every day. So much concentration was required to take into account the length of the lorry at those dreaded roundabouts and tight turns, and every evening I'd wonder whether I would ever manage it. I was so glad of clean mirrors, reversing cameras, and rubber points on the lorry, but even then, a few times the set cones that were marked out seemed to disappear!

It helped that I hadn't planned to have any riding lessons at night, because I was like a bear with a sore head when I got home every evening from that course. Having Sesky to ride for a while, though, helped me to destress, and was a great way to finish the day.

I battled on through the week, and on the Saturday morning at 8am, Pat met me at the Test Centre and presented me with my lorry. I just shrank as I saw the examiner walking towards me with his clipboard; he was the one guy I had hoped I would not get, so my dreaded day was already off to a bad start!

Once I had confidently finished all my vehicle checks, I was allowed into the lorry to do my adjustments, then we were off around the Test Centre to various points. This involved carrying out different manoeuvres, answering questions, and then tackling the dreaded reversing. The examiner told me that he required the lorry to be reversed to the exact line and, having practised this many a time with Pat, I knew exactly what 'to the line' meant. Using my little marker point on the lorry with mirrors, all the cones were still standing, and to the exact line was exactly what he got. Job complete! I had a brief smile to myself as I remembered the days when my young son would hide behind the seat when I was reversing.

The emergency stop could have seen the lorry squash up from rear to front, as I did it exactly on the hit of the clipboard to the dashboard, and we were stopped before the examiner could lift it back up again. I could now breathe, knowing that I had passed that part, then he told me to 'head out to the road'. Now all I had to do was to drive this lorry as if I drove it every day.

The roads were surprisingly busy for a Saturday morning, but I just kept thinking it would soon be over. I followed his directions to the letter, then – sweating – returned to the Test Centre and was told to park up and turn the engine off. With not even a smile on his face, he scribbled his pen across his clipboard while I imagined the worst, then he duly turned and handed the paper to me with the words, 'You've passed', and gave me a slight smile and nod as we left the lorry. When he'd left, I spotted Pat in the parking bay, and ran across with sheer delight to tell her the good news.

Driving my car seemed more difficult than the lorry, and I was shaking as I made my way back to the yard, but I could not wait to wave my pass certificate in the air to tell everyone. Even Sesky got a look at it. I had completed another big challenge, so I could now relax, although I'd hang on to the theory book for future reference.

It took me that full week to settle down, although the thought of driving the six-horse HGV Lorry was now firmly on my mind. I was excited at the prospect of not having to make double trips any more.

*

What an exciting time it had been! Tsunami had started her showjumping career at the shows; I was fully riding Sesky again; Copper had her new foal; and my HGV training was completed and passed. And we were still only halfway through the year.

Sesky and I were having the time of our lives, enjoying lots of treks with the clients, with her as my main trek leading horse. We both enjoyed the longer routes and the lively canters back in across the fields with the horses and ponies, even on wet days. When the more novice treks went out, Sesky had time in the field or to relax before our special riding time at the end of each day.

She seemed fitter now than she had been for a while, and was still full of energy and character on most days. I was always eager for the opportunity to take her away into the countryside and be back before the evening lessons, or to wander off together for hours on my time off, when there was no need to rush back. These rides gave us the chance to see the summer and autumn nights at their best, where Loch Lomond shone like a diamond within the countryside, and I was determined not to waste any precious time.

The month of September that year (2007), though, was one of the wettest I can remember, with the water running down the roads and out of the fields like rivers. I had organised a sponsored walk for the ILPH (International League for the Protection of Horses) with the school clients – most of them incredibly young – and it was a day when I could have done with being mounted up on Sesky instead of being on my own two feet. She would have loved the water, but she was nicely tucked up in the stable while we marched on. The heavens opened that day, and we were all soaked to the skin from early on. But we waded our way around the roads and countryside, determined not to give up, and raised an incredible £3000 for the ILPH/ Hoof It For

Horses campaign. The cheque was proudly presented to the Hoof It For Horses mascot, who came out to meet us all, and we proudly wore our Hoof It T-shirts for the photographs.

I was now driving the HGV lorry around as though I had done it for years, without a second thought about the size of it. I have to admit, though, the tight turns in and out of some places did take a good bit of consideration and thought before being tackled. When the air suspension went down on arrival at the shows, it was like a sigh of relief that we had got there with all the horses and the lorry unscratched! On one occasion, the satnav on the mobile phone took us in the wrong direction, and I was left doing about an eight-point turn on the road before a low bridge, but I managed to leave the field fence still standing and the gate untouched as I smiled and thanked the drivers who were patiently waiting to pass. I left wondering what they were thinking, though I was secretly quite impressed with myself. I was just glad Sesky was not on the lorry that day, with all the commotion.

A few years later, the BHS brought out the new coaching qualification which I'd heard about. Determined not to be left behind, I made a few enquiries and, before I knew it, I had booked myself on the course that lasted several months. *What had I done?* The notes and files grew bigger, the studying was harder, and the away training and assessment days seemed never-ending and longer each time. Some days I hardly had time to sit on Sesky, far less go for a calming ride. I had thought my exam days were over, and yet here I was throwing myself back in when I did not really need to.

Coaching nights and feedback sessions were done everywhere with anyone available, and included a few on myself, so I soon had my files complete and was prepared for exam day. For some reason, it felt worse than doing my HGV study and test. But the outcome was the same, and I passed my UKCC Generic Coaching in March 2009. When my certificate arrived, I decided that was the last exam I would take. I was now satisfied to be part of the new Coaching Qualification, and all that stress, long hours of studying, taking notes, and coaching with assessments, had finally paid off.

My time was finally my own again to spend with Sesky, and I could ride her until my heart was content.

Throughout life, I guess we can prepare and plan for some things, but not all. I was certainly not prepared for what happened one morning in October 2010 when I went to collect Adonis and Chester from the field. They had recently been spending only every second night or so out in the field, to prepare them for coming inside for the winter months. The weather had until then been good, but we'd had one or two surprising late-night frosts, with a little bit still lying in the morning that caught us out.

Adonis and Chester, now six years old, had been happily in and out of work for some time, and in recent months had taken part in a few Intro Showjumping competitions, showing a lot of potential. Adonis, in partic-ular, had jumped clear in only his second time in the ring, and a few other times after that. Now they were being left to mature for the next spring shows beginning.

But that morning was to be like no other. As soon as I set eyes on Adonis, I knew he was not right. Although he looked fabulous, just like Chester, the sparkle was gone from him. His eyes were dull, and he did not run to the gate as he would normally do when I arrived. There was a huge difference from the horse that had been turned out the night before.

As he walked to the stable, he looked so lethargic that I knew the vet should be called. And by the time he arrived, Adonis was even worse, and quite distressed. After examination, the vet said that he assumed Adonis had Acute Grass Sickness. I could hardly believe this. I had read about the study which the vet school in Edinburgh had done on grass sickness, and knew how serious it was. It meant that Adonis was going to die, or would need put down within a few days, as horses did not survive from this. If it had been the Chronic Grass Sickness, he might have stood a better chance!

I was in total shock. This was Sesky's youngster, and I was about to lose him. After long discussions with the vet, and with no time to waste, it was decided that Adonis would be driven to the vet school. Our vet would make him comfortable for the journey, and the vet school would have some time to do their checks on him. It would help them with their studies, too, so it would not all be for nothing.

It was a hard decision to make, and I knew I could not do the journey with him myself. Within two days, I got the phone call to say Adonis had been put to sleep, and the vet school thanked me for the opportunity they'd had to see him. All my little scribbles of things I noted down, regarding the change of weather, etc, had seemed like a daft habit, but it provided useful information for the researchers when we were discussing the situation on the phone.

It was a sad day in the yard and, being unexpected, it was a real shock. Passing the empty stable where he had once stood was soul-destroying for a long time. The days and the work had to carry on, though, and I threw myself into the lessons and treks as my way of dealing with it, and pampered Sesky even more than normal. Thankfully, none of the other horses or ponies on the yard came down with it, so how and why it happened remained a mystery. However, it was a topic that I used in the Stable Management training, handing out leaflets which I had got from the vet school and, sadly, explaining about our own hands-on experience with Adonis.

After many years of providing us with excellent care for the horses and ponies (for which I am eternally grateful), Jim had retired from being a farrier, although I still had a little job for him to do from time to time. Unknown to the older riders in the school who were going through their TRSS qualifications and riding exams with me, I had arranged that Jim would come in and examine them on their grades, as he was a BHS AI. Jim would come along, dressed for the occasion in his professional riding attire, and I think it was a competition between him and me on the day to see which one of us had the shiniest long riding boots on!

He was taken into the school and, as they stood with their horses and ponies, I introduced him as Mr Fraser, their examiner for the day, while Jim and I tried not to laugh. They did not recognise him as the farrier who had looked after all the horses and ponies they stood with, and who had previously given them farrier talks in the past. These training and exam days were long and hard work over the years for everyone, but they were always full of enjoyment. A lot of the riders gained their much-wanted TRSS Achievement Awards, and looked forward to a restful night when they could reflect on their achievements and I could reflect on my days, but…

When all your work is finished, and you sit alone and wonder where time goes, you realise how true the saying is that 'time waits for no-one'. Life continually changes and circumstances seem different, but you just get up and carry on, sometimes burying your head in the sand and not wanting to face the truth as the easiest way to deal with things.

With the children all grown up, I questioned what I had left if all the horses, etc, were taken out of the picture. I finally had to face up to whether being married on paper and being myself was really how I wanted to remain, knowing that we had drifted apart over the years.

I kept myself busy, over and above riding Sesky, and decided with a friend that we would take part in Scotland's first ever Shine Walk for cancer, which was being held in Glasgow the following year. In preparation, we started building up our walking days round the countryside to be ready to tackle the half marathon. When the midnight walk came around, we took to the streets of Glasgow with about another three thousand people, lights glowing, as we marched around the streets. It was another time when I thought it would have been handy for Sesky to have been there to give us a lift and save our tired legs!

A few hours later, we were glad to see that finish line and to collect our medal at the other side, showing we had completed it.

As I climbed into bed for a few hours' sleep, I realised how daft I had been to organise training on the yard the following day!

As Sesky no longer took part in meetings and competitions, I came up with a few other crazy ideas. Giving some free rides at the village celebration was quite enjoyable, with the school ponies doing their part for the riders, walking along the country lane quite happily.

And we again gave free pony rides at one of the local shopping centres Loch Lomond Shores on their tenth anniversary celebration, at which HRH Princess Anne had come to unveil one of the statues at Loch Lomond. I was given the honour of being introduced to her as she came to admire the ponies and mention her love for horses. I took the opportunity to proudly mention the age of Sesky and how she was still in work, wishing she had been there to be shown off.

Me with Princess Anne 2012
Photo Credit: © Mirrorpix/Reach Licencing.

One big idea in which Sesky did get a chance to take part, was my Brave Challenge at the riding school. The Scottish Tourist Board had invited businesses to set up a challenge for tourists, similar to the *Brave* movie, and being a Four Star-approved Centre by them, I was determined to take up the challenge!

With lots of help and planning, I organised costumes and fun activities throughout the weekends of July and August, including archery, horseback riding, and hours of fun. Sesky was my trek leading horse as we took out the experienced riders on their horses or ponies on their 'eventful rides', and she would be prancing about as we passed all the activity coming back in. She was and always will be my little Braveheart.

It was nice to get back to normal after a busy year or two, and Sesky was still as fit as ever at the incredible age of 26 years young in 2012. No-one could believe she could still give them a good run for their money out round the treks or while having a canter back in across the fields, but she was still full of energy and looked totally fabulous. She had always loved her exercise and riding, and it did not look like that was going to change any time soon. She would always look at me as I walked up early in the morning, her ears pricked up as if to say 'Now will do, Mother' as I walked past with the ponies' tack for the lessons or treks.

And even though I was fond of all the horses and ponies, I always preferred spending time riding Sesky – something I managed to do most days. We'd have a short warm-up in the school first, to make sure we both were ready for wherever we ended up, then we'd head off on one of our favourite routes, with some canters in the fields thrown in to use up some energy. As the shorter days and the winter nights approached, we tried to ride before lunch if the ground was not icy outside, because the teaching went into the later part of the evening. Having weekends at home with a quiet yard was great fun, and as the time was our own, Sesky could be pampered and ridden until our hearts were content. If the ground in the field was frozen or not suitable for going out, she could have a free run in the school to have a few bucks and broncos to let off steam while she ran snorting to the gates. She was not one to like being left in the stable for a period, as she got fed up – just like me, I guess. She was always happier out and enjoying our riding.

It was always a joy to see the springtime coming, with the lighter nights and longer days. And once the weather improved, we could get back out in the countryside once again and enjoy some freedom from the schoolwork. When she got her full clip – even though it made her lively – it was the sign that we were fully ready to go round our longer routes, with lots of trotting and canters across the fields without her being covered in sweat. It always took her a few days to settle down when being ridden after clipping, especially if it got windy and we were round the road at the top of the hill. When the wind got 'up her tail', I often thought we would never slow down at the other side! Having some sheep racing in the field next to us made it even worse, as she thought she should catch up along the road. On those days, I would be glad I had no clients with us. With a firm seat in the saddle, no traffic nearby, and my good grip riding gloves on, I was sorted!

Chapter 11

Transition

'Hot to Trot'

The year of 2014 might have been the 20th Anniversary of my Riding School & Trekking Centre, which I had long looked forward to, but it turned out to be a year from hell; a year in which I personally had to change.

I remember thinking back to a time when I was probably about 12 years old, and I'd asked myself, 'If life is what makes you happy, then what else do you need?' Back then, I'd thought the answer was simply 'my feet, determination, and health'. But I had now realised that a lot of that happiness had slipped away!

I'd experienced enjoyment and contentment with horses, work, and a bit of family life, but loneliness for a long, long time had been and was now staring me in the face – something I had not wanted to acknowledge. It felt as though everyone had moved on with their lives – some creating new ones – while I was left in the nightmare of a black hole, feeling so low that I knew I needed to get out.

I guess they say that 'to find happiness, you need to find yourself first', and it is something I had given a fair bit of thought to over several years. Delving deep into dark, lonely places, I finally knew I wanted to – indeed had to – change my life.

So, that year, I started to change my thoughts about myself and looking after me! And the following year, I made a dramatic change in my life. After a lot of heartache and soul-searching, I had decided what I wanted, and that Sesky and I had to ride out of the yard… but this time, without returning.

That early cold February morning was one I could never have imagined. With my car and few possessions already taken off the yard, I then rode Sesky away on our last journey from there. This time, she did not have a choice where to go at the dirt track; we had to go straight on. I think Sesky carried me along the road that day, as I just sat there, totally numb. But I had made my decision, and I was sticking to it.

It was such a long, cold trek, with the icy snow still lying on the grass verge from previous days, and it was the only time I ever wished our ride would soon come to an end. My mind was just a blur, and with ground conditions so tricky at points, I was just desperate to get to her new barn, which would be her stable area.

On turning the last corner on the long road ahead, I lifted my head and looked up to see slight sunshine glimmering in the gaps between the wintry sky, as if to say, 'You're almost there.' By the time I finally dismounted, I was so cold I could not feel my feet, and Sesky was not that warm either.

Shaki and I had a friendship that grew into a relation-ship, and he had made up a stable area for Sesky in part of his barn. Now that we had arrived, my challenge was to get Sesky in there. The place was so quiet, apart from the odd noise from the cows in the other shed. When she heard them, Sesky stopped suddenly in her tracks, the only thing on her mind being that there was no way she was moving. It was freezing and I needed to get her inside and warmed up, but after a while, it was useless, and I would need help. With no-one around, the phone call was made and, luckily enough, Shaki was nearby. He helped to block her so that she had to move forward, and eventually she ran in, with a few pulls from me to stop her jumping the gate at the back and out again. I grabbed the front gate to close it, holding onto her tightly, while Shaki disappeared, away from this crazy horse, shaking his head!

The stable area was soon like a steam room. with Sesky spinning around and snorting liked a crazy stallion, while I tried to untack her. Having to concentrate on her kept my mind off my own situation, as I tried to settle her down. I dried her off, even though she had been clipped, and rugged her up before leaving her to settle while I nipped out to bring more straw in.

She continued to pound round the stable area, rushing forward and barging the gate every time she heard the cows, and it took her a long time to settle. I guess passing them in the fields was completely different to having them nearby. They were probably wondering what all the neigh-ing and snorting noise was from their new neighbour, too.

I parked my car right across her outside door so that I could keep a close eye on her, and went to warm up in the car. Later, Shaki took her a nice fresh bale of haylage, which

Sesky usually loved the smell of. She would normally grab the net before it could be hung up in the stable. But on this occasion, she was not interested in the slightest, and just nudged it with her head then marched around, knocking her water bucket over as she passed.

As she was clearly unsettled at the strange surroundings, I thought a nice groom over might settle her down, with nice warm rugs on, and a bucket of warm bran wash with some apples and carrots. I also placed a radio nearby to distract her, but she was still not interested in her haylage, and the bucket of food was trampled into the ground with hardly any eaten.

The evening came quickly, and as daylight disappeared, Sesky stood at the gate looking a little more settled than earlier. She had eaten a mouthful or two of haylage, and she walked round the stable area and back to the gate, with her head hung over, not interested in much while I went in and out from the car that night to check her.

When morning broke, I was in with her, changing her net to give her fresh haylage and some extra on the straw to encourage her to nibble. I tried another warm bucket of bran mash, which was normally her favourite to eat, but it stood untouched. Deciding I might hand feed her with it, I squeezed it into her mouth, but most of it fell back onto the floor. Eventually, I decided a phone call to the vet was needed for reassurance. I continued to hand feed her with the bran mash that day with a little bit of feed in it, willing her to eat more, and constantly watching her for the slightest bit of change. A mouthful or two of water was drunk, with the rest splashed about.

It was just as well the cows were there to save wastage and eat all the haylage that was taken back out uneaten.

Sesky never liked the same nets left in at any time if she had not eaten them, so I tried to explain this to Shaki – whose real name is David – but I'm sure it never made any sense to him, and he just shook his head. (And, no, I have never understood his nickname either!)

Another long night passed, with me in and out checking her, trying to encourage her to eat. I tried another warm bucket of bran mash in the early hours of the morning with some feed, and as the light broke the sky, she slowly started to eat it herself. I was ecstatic, and ran in to wake up Shaki to tell him. His face was a picture when he realised the time, as he still had a few hours before he needed to milk at the dairy.

I knew now she was on the mend, and when I was mucking her out a little later, she nibbled the fresh net slowly from time to time, which was a great relief. With fresh water, a nice groom over, and rugs changed, she eventually stood happily munching her haylage. Later, when Shaki came back from the dairy that morning and came in to offer her a carrot, she grabbed it out of his hand. Looking quite pleased with himself, he headed off to breakfast – and so did I. After the worry and stress of the last few days, I reckoned I deserved it.

With no income, I realised I could not dwell on my situation and would need to find a job. I had a horse to look after, and I had to live. Later that day in the paper, we spotted an advert for a Trek Leader in a small riding centre not too far away, so I decided to call, and was offered an interview the next day.

Thankfully, the interview went well, and that week I worked for a few days to assist treks and get to know the place and surroundings, as well as the horses and ponies.

It was great to have a job and to keep my mind off things. The following days, taking some treks out with an assistant, felt great. Finishing early was better still, and I would rush back to Sesky mid-afternoon to find some bits of carrot lying about, and knew Shaki, or someone, had paid her a visit. The job seemed great, although there were some long days when the trekking was busy, then mucking in with everyone until the yard was finished for the night, and staying while needed. I was not afraid of a hard day's work, especially at that time of year when everything was cold, wet, and muddy as we headed out of winter and into spring. We made the most out of what treks we could do, though some were not so enjoyable as we walked through the muddy fields.

I was not needed the first weekend after starting at the centre, which was great. And after helping a bit at the dairy with Shaki, I decided I would get Sesky out for a ride, as she had been in the stable all week to let her settle in. When I finished her mucking out and she was finally ready and tacked up, she stood... and she stood... and would not move an inch out of her stable area, no matter how hard I tried. After quite some time, once again I had to see if someone was nearby to help me get her out. Eventually, with help, a bit of pushing, pulling, and a wave from the whip behind, she shot out of the barn door, dragging me with her – but at least she was out!

Grabbing my chair to mount up, I was quickly on her, and she was spinning around outside, finally prancing down the drive out of the farm, snorting loudly like a crazy, fresh horse. We headed to the area across the road where the haylage bales were stored, and I used it as my braking point to try and slow her down. No way was I attempting the country roads!

Choosing to stay in this area to get her calmer, we jogged about for quite some time, with the tail high in the air. I knew it was going to take quite a while, but thankfully we had all day. Eventually, with my arms aching, we could just about manage a jogging walk down there and around about the other farm buildings, and after a few good hours she finally settled, with the reins being relaxed a bit.

Later, I managed to ride her back over and up the drive again to her stable, with a little bit of prancing about, and with a bit of gentle persuasion she rushed back into her bed. Glad to see her hay net for a good rub and scratch, she stood there like a little angel, while I was the one who was exhausted, hot, and bothered.

With the fields being big and her not easy to catch, I decided the best option was for her to stay inside just now, or she would be out with the cows forever. So, plenty of pulled grass was put in the buckets for her, and we soon got a routine of going in and out more calmly, and eventually ventured around the country roads on the days when I finished work a bit earlier. I also made a few trips to my mum's house to bring back some spare quilts to keep her cosy under the rugs, and she seemed much happier.

I took her out one morning for a long ride, and came back after a few hours, happy that she had been really good and that no visit to the bale area was needed to calm her down. But as we walked back up the drive, at the side of the shed, she suddenly slammed the brakes on, started spinning and snorting on the spot, tail in the air, and bolted back down the drive. I had no choice but to run her straight across into the bale area to stop her, screaming 'Sesky!'

madly at her. When we finally headed back up the drive and were almost to the top, I was unable to get her anywhere near the corner. After a long time of trying, I once again had to call for assistance, and she was ushered to her barn with the help of the Jeep parked across the drive to stop her running back, and some encouragement from me. It was only when I had finally dismounted right outside her stable and taken her in that I realised the sheep were in the barn for lambing, and she must have been spooked when she sensed them as we came up the drive.

Now I had another job on my hands a few times each day, encouraging her to at least come out of the stable. With her bridle on and the car parked across the drive to stop her running off, she was led back and forward past the sheep until she got used to them. When she stood quite happily munching the haylage from the bale outside, watching them, I realised my job was done, although she could still be a little jumpy some days when the little lambs were running about.

The job at the Trekking Centre was good while it lasted, but they had been unable to give me the full-time hours I needed, and part-time was no good for me. I phoned a larger equestrian centre I knew that might be looking for staff, and after a few phone calls and an interview, I started a day or two later as a stable hand. Being back in amongst all the horses again was super, as it was a really large stable yard with showjumping competitions, a riding academy, and country club. It really was an amazing place and I quickly settled into the different hours and shifts, despite a bit of a journey back and forward to work.

Knowing which were my working days was much easier than the job before, and having a pay packet in my hand at the end of it was extremely satisfying. Being able to do some teaching from time to time just made everything so much better.

When I had lunchtime starts, I could feed the cows next to Sesky early, finish her off, help Shaki a bit in the dairy, ride out if I wanted, then head to work. On early morning starts, it was cows and Sesky sorted, then fly off to work. Leaving Sesky on the long shifts was horrible, because I was used to her being with me, but I knew she would be fine and that someone would pop in to give her a carrot. Watching the cows in the field behind her barn kept her amused until I returned, then I'd waste no time in having her ready for riding.

In those days she would still come out of the stable jogging around before I was seated, and marching down the drive before I was ready. The odd leap forward would be thrown in, as the lambs were jumping in the air and running around in the fields, or if she decided to race the cows in the field as they started running because her prancing around had unsettled them. I just needed stamina and strength to keep up with her, especially after a hard day's work.

We jogged and pranced along the country roads almost every day, with a few sideways steps onto the grass verges as she got more excited when the tractors passed. Shaki would just give a shake of the head at how crazy she was. Give him cows over horses any day!

Sesky still seemed like that young lively horse she had been when she was four years old, despite the fact that she was now 29 years young! I guess it's a true saying that age is only a number, and you are as young as you feel. There was certainly no sign of her retiring any time soon, as she

Shaki's cows relaxing in the sunshine.

always thrived on her work. She still looked forward to that canter in the field as the ground improved, no matter how long we had been out riding for. And most of the time we were out, she stayed in trot – although, some days it was more like jogging!

As the springtime came and the weather improved, our rides out did, too, and we managed longer routes for a few hours on my days off. And when that led into summer, the long clear nights after work offered plenty of chance for relaxing rides once Sesky had eventually calmed down – about 40 minutes into our ride. We'd return contented sometime later, with her happily walking calmly into her stable, looking forward to her haylage and feed.

On a summer's day she enjoyed nothing better than to be standing out the back in the sunshine, tied up, being bathed, and munching the haylage bale near her. On our early morning rides before I went to work, she would be bouncing with energy as we left. But when she had to be turned around at a spot before venturing too far, she would show her disapproval at having to end her ride early, by briskly trotting back with the tail swishing. On some days she was so disgruntled that we had to pay the bales a visit to calm her down and stop her taking off. Without a doubt, she always kept me awake and on my toes.

On the summer mornings, I loved being out at about five o'clock to see to Sesky and pop into the cows beside her to feed them, before going to work early. But nothing could have been nicer than one morning when I got a glimpse of a little calf being born in the field as I walked towards the barn. Forgetting about Sesky, I ran and climbed over the gate, then made my way slowly towards the cow, trying not to frighten her. Thankfully, the calf had just been born, as I might not have been much help if it was stuck! Running back across the field, I scrambled over the gate, running into the house, throwing the door open to wake Shaki up, and shouting to him that a Belta calf had just been born and he had to come and see it. As he had already been out in the early hours to check the cows as normal, there was no doubt a shake of the head followed at his sleep being interrupted!

Belta cows was one of my favourite breeds, with the black body and the broad white band around their middle. They just looked so cute, and this little calf was the image of its mum. From then on, I always laughed and joked that this calf was mine because I had seen it first and witnessed its birth.

That summer was a bit mixed, with a few heavy days of rain which seemed to never stop. Sesky, though, was in her glory, as she splashed about the puddles as she trotted along the roads. On extremely wet days we missed out the fields and the canters, but we still enjoyed being out and about together despite being soaked.

After the long, unbelievably wet days of being in the stable, when Sesky was finally back out she was like a surge of power as we travelled along the roads. And it wasn't long until the sun made its appearance, giving us the rest of the summer to enjoy being back in the field and allowing her to canter until her heart was content.

With helping Shaki and everyone at the dairy, and watching what went on with the milking and the calves, I got an idea of how hard the work was. Looking after the chickens, and collecting the eggs was certainly a whole lot easier... until I tried to clean out their feet! Catching them was similar to getting hold of Sesky, and on a good day it took several attempts!

I was glad to be able to spend some evenings pottering about in the garden, to relax and admire some of the flowers in full bloom, when my work was done with Sesky.

The new job was going well, and I'd settled into the routine. I'd also added the new title of BHS Accredited

Flowers in the garden.

Professional Coach to my qualifications, so was feeling pretty pleased with myself. As the autumn months began to creep in, I was proudly wearing my BHS jacket, displaying the professional coach logo and my name, while teaching privately. I was doing a lot more teaching in the academy, so my hours would vary. It was a busy yard, and as I had my HGV licence, I often drove their lorry to pick up horses or for any visits to the vet school for clients. It was great to get behind the wheel of the lorry again, even though this one was slightly longer than the one I used to drive. I drove it around the large lorry park and yard for a bit to get used to it, but all went well when I went on my first drive out, and it meant I could add another job to my list.

With the number of facilities and opportunities there, I was thinking about the fast-approaching winter – and Sesky. With the dark nights soon to be upon us, I knew our riding would be limited. And if the weather was not suitable in the mornings to go out before work, or if it was icy, we might not get out at all!

The fresh sharp autumn mornings and cooler days and nights saw Sesky come out of her stable like a tense stallion, eager to get moving. And on some days, she would take off as we rode along the roads. On the nights when I finished work a bit later, it was difficult to get a decent ride out for long before darkness descended, so riding times and routes had to be well planned.

I had a serious decision to consider regarding where Sesky would spend the winter, though. While Shaki had been great to give us somewhere to stay, I had to move her to somewhere which was better suited. Ingliston Country Club in Bishopton, where I worked, had the choice of two large outdoor riding arenas, with all-weather surfaces, floodlighting, two indoor riding schools, a horse walker, solariums, paddocks, and stables to choose from, so there was no question where her new home should be. Once I'd decided, and had made sure everything was ready for Sesky at her new home, Iona picked her up one day with me and we took her to the new place.

Chapter 12

Pastures New

Sesky came off the lorry as fast as I had ever seen her, and thankfully Iona had a hold of her, not me. She stood like a giraffe, spinning around constantly, and neighing with excitement as she saw the other horses and ponies and all the activity going on. Thank goodness her stable was ready, and we put her in quickly before she had other ideas!

Once inside, she jumped around the stable, neighing at everyone and anything that moved, as if to announce her arrival. And with all the other horses and ponies alerted to the disturbance she was causing, it was quite a noisy time. She took quite a while to settle down, so it was probably just as well I was not working that day.

I had picked out the stable that would be easiest and most convenient for me to handle Sesky when she was lively, and probably the safest option, too. She was just in from the middle entrance, out of the wind, round the turn, right next to the wash bay with solarium lights above, which could also be used for clipping. Her stable was also near to the feed room, so convenient for my early morning feeds, and with the rug room close by. And most important-ly, it was also not too far from the dung heap, for dumping that wheelbarrow!

The tack room was opposite, and only a few steps away, and there was only a short walk to the indoor schools, through the corridors, and not too far to the outdoor arenas either. We had everything we could dream of, so all I needed now was for her to settle down and relax.

With most of the paddocks closing soon for the winter, I was glad that I did not need to worry about turning her out until the spring, and there was the possibility she could go back to Shaki's then. In the meantime, she would have the arenas outside to have a good run about in.

Within no time at all Sesky had settled into her new routine and home, and there was no problem with her eating habits this time, although I think she preferred Shaki's good haylage! After her isolation period, she enjoyed a great free blast about in the outdoor arena, enjoy-ing the nice rubber surface as she galloped about bucking and showing off, while I watched her as I stood guarding the gate. A few days of this, with me hanging onto the rope as she jogged to the arena, took the edge off her, and soon she was ready to ride in a quieter frame of mind. Or so I thought.

After work, as there were no lessons on, I chose to use the smaller indoor school to ride for our first time, but Sesky had other ideas. Walking around, she passed by the large windows of the restaurant, which was situated just at the edge of the walkway beside the schools. Having never seen anything like this before, she was soon snorting, pran-cing round on high steps, tail in the air once again, and eyes popping out of her head! Let's just say, that first night was exciting, and several times I thought I was nearly coming off.

Sesky eventually got used to the indoor schools, and all the movement at the windows and restaurant, and soon she was working around, not bothering. In saying that, she loved all the attention when people would come around the arena walls to watch everyone ride, and she would automatically stop at them, looking for that pat and attention she used to get from the tourists, standing quite happily to be admired as we chatted. Some days and nights she would need nudged on quite a bit, to let her know that she had stopped often enough and that she was to work on.

The soft surfaces were amazing for riding on, and she really enjoyed her lively canters and once again riding with the different horses and ponies in the school. On some nights, when the jumps were out in the larger schools and some of the other horses were jumping, it was pretty clear that Sesky hoped we would be joining in. I wondered if perhaps I had unleashed the dragon in her once again, but I swiftly passed on any such idea and kept her away.

A nice calm walk around the quiet arenas on a loose rein after working, would see her stop at the door when she was satisfied and finished. Then she would be tucked up in bed to rest for the night... and I wasn't long behind her.

The year of 2016 was an exciting and massively eventful one. Sesky, now 30 years old and still full of spirit and looking fabulous, had a big birthday to celebrate. Apart from getting a sparkling diamante brow band, which was specially chosen and made, she was about to move into a new luxury stable.

One day, late in the afternoon, while I was working, I was summoned to the owners' main office, but I had no idea why. To my surprise, and delight, I was offered the position as Academy Manager, which would involve doing all the teaching, and moving off the normal duties in the livery yard. I was now going to be doing the job I had once loved, and running the Riding School section. As I was to get a pay rise, there was only one thing on my mind. And as soon as I left the meeting, I was determined that Sesky was now going to have the best I could get her. Straight away, I picked out her stable from two available in the main Full Livery Gold barn, and put her onto her new full livery just in time for her birthday, which was a few weeks away in the middle of February.

I was so thrilled. The new stable was next to the side entrance, beside the huge sliding doors, and would allow her to look out at the walkway and private road to keep her amused, and getting lots of fresh air when she was inside, while the doors would be closed over for comfort at night. I wanted to prepare her stable, even though she was on full livery. So, along with thick rubber matting on the floor, she got a nice big bed of shavings on top, and haylage nets tied up. Her hay rack had some, too, although she was not used to these. Even though it had water drinkers in, Sesky was not familiar with these either, and preferred her water bucket. The stable was beautiful, with a nice sliding door, shiny wood finishing, and brass balls around the top of the stable bars. It looked fit for a princess, and exactly where Sesky belonged. Sesky was walked briskly around, and was soon rolling in her new posh stable! And I was grinning from ear to hear when she stood admiring the view outside, giving the neigh of approval.

With my new position in the academy, most nights involved teaching until late into the evenings, but now I knew Sesky would be well looked after on full livery. As I had school horses and ponies to get ready before teaching in the mornings, I no longer needed to panic about getting Sesky done first on these early starts.

I was grateful to be allowed the choice of two private paddocks for putting Sesky out. These normally opened in the springtime, but I was given permission for her to go out on her own, as she was one of the oldest horses there and was not good with other horses. Everything was perfect, but I must have been one of the worst full livery clients there was, giving my strict instructions for Sesky about the way I liked everything for her, even down to the colour of her hay nets to be used for morning and night. It took me a long time to settle into the full livery world.

Sesky was enjoying herself and going out nicely for the staff to the paddock and back in for her lunch, pretending to be an angel. She was happy, and that was the most important thing. When I finished my working day, I still had time to spend grooming, riding, and just having quality time with Sesky. Skipping her bed out last thing at night, and finishing her off, always made me feel as though I was doing my bit, too. On my days off, we'd spend time riding in the school, then go out and explore the new countryside. Some days we covered a good eight-mile route, with lively Sesky still wanting her canters in the school on our return.

It was such a pleasure not to worry about all the mucking out with Sesky, and even the bathing and clipping was done to perfection, the way I liked it. Sesky loved every minute of standing under the solarium lights, drying off in the heat as she munched her haylage beside her. I loved walking through the barn from the academy, between lessons, and seeing her standing there shining like a diamond and happy as could be. It always brightened up my day. And with her stable being close to the indoor school, I was forever nipping in to say hi and getting a neigh back as I walked through the connecting corridors.

Driving back and forward when I finished with Sesky, and getting used to my new position in the academy, I felt as though everything in my life was falling into place. I was always eager to find out from Shaki if I had missed any new lambs or calves being born while I'd been away at work, and to hear about his busy day. The showjumping competitions, which were held at the centre most week-ends, gave the place that extra buzz and filled the gap from what I had been missing, and I enjoyed watching them on my time off.

Sesky was always amused on these days as she watched from her stable while all the horses and ponies trotted by, enjoying the attention when some people stopped to see her at the doorway. There were some friendly faces she had not seen for a long time, and there was never a dull moment for her. On the late-night finishes, I loved to check in on her before heading off, with only the sound of horses happily munching to send me on my way. Then I'd return in the early morning to slide the door open and be greeted by Sesky's neighing sound as she eagerly looked at me, and for her breakfast. It was a great way to start the day.

We had lots of lovely rides out as the weather improved, and were finding our way around all different routes along country roads. As there were no off-road riding routes, we missed the canters in the fields we used to have at Shaki's, but the huge school and outdoor arenas gave her the opportunity to burn off steam. Even being out in the paddocks on most days, she still had loads of energy at the end of our rides. She was such an incredible little horse for her age.

That summer on the yard saw quite a few trips to the beach at Irvine for some people, with the lorries being loaded up, but I always seemed to be working on those days, so I missed out. One day, however, a few friends and I finally got together and organised a day to the beach when we were all off together. Sesky had never been anywhere like that for years so, with the lorry prepared the night before, we headed off early the next morning. Sesky ran up the ramp of the lorry behind the other two horses so that she would be off first, and the door quickly closed before she had any other ideas.

As I was not driving, I could nip through the lorry and check on her during the journey, but she was fine, and stood happily munching with the others. I had wanted to go to the beach again for such a long time but never had the chance, so I was really excited about the trip.

When we arrived, we got them ready and off the lorry, then, with a quick mount up, the three of us were ready and bouncing down to the sand, eager to get there first. The three horses were loving the sea air and slight breeze on such a nice sunny day, so it looked like they were going to give us a challenge. Sesky, although a lot older than the other two, kept up with them as we jogged along the beach then broke into trot, covering a good distance. Then, with all legs coming high up as they got faster, we were into a canter. It certainly blew off the cobwebs that day!

It felt as though we had cantered for miles, before we slowed down and enjoyed a lovely walk through the water, Sesky splashing as she jumped about with excitement. It was such a lovely way to cool us all down in the sunshine, and this time my seat was firmly in the saddle and my feet glued to my stirrups; I was not coming off!

As we played about the beach for a good while, trotting in and out of the water and along the sand, we decided on another short gallop… or maybe it was the horses that decided! That's when everything about that good position went into the air, and we charged along the beach, all hanging onto the horses' necks, giggling and laughing at having such a great time, especially as the beach was almost empty. We could have stayed there all day and night; it was such fun. I had a chuckle to myself that at least the jellyfish had not got Sesky and me this time, and I was thrilled that I had managed to stay mounted.

The journey back to the yard was full of giggles as we chatted about our amazing day at the beach; it was something I would never forget. That night I looked proudly at Sesky as I left her snuggled up in her stable. It had been a lovely way to finish off the summer.

The autumn months gave us the luxury to choose whether to ride in or out, or to wander around the centre itself in the walkways between the paddocks and large parking areas. Both outdoor arenas were still allowing the rides outside as the nights drew in, but the bright lights sometimes spooked Sesky when she caught sight of her own shadow as she trotted around.

The winter did not only bring the dull days and nights, but it also brought the unexpected dark news that the Riding Academy was being closed to make way for other business ideas. I was devastated, as I'd had no idea that this was happening, and it was hard to take in. I was offered a job in the housekeeping department in the accommodation side of the business, as they needed staff, and I accepted without hesitation. I needed a job, and didn't fancy going back to being a stable hand full-time. I felt I had done my fair share of that in all the years I'd had horses.

The hours and days off in the new job suited me well, as there were no constant late-night finishes, so I could still do freelance teaching with people I had taught privately before, and at different yards, and it gave me more time with Sesky. The huge drop in pay was something I could have done without, but I had no option. The main thing was that Sesky would still stay on her full livery, as she deserved the best and I was not for changing that. *Beans and toast will feed me anytime!* I thought.

The housekeeping job was not something I would have thought about in the past, although I had always enjoyed my own housework and had taken great pride in it. This job was completely different, though, and so much harder. But I knuckled down and got on with it.

I met a lot of new people that I had seen passing by while I was riding, but I had never worked with them before. I was now in a new team of workers, and this is where I met Agnes, who became a good friend. Any time we were going to clean the lodges or to do jobs there, I always made sure to go via the stable block, to have a peek in at Sesky and say hi. But I walked extra quickly, honest! On our breaks, we wandered past her, too, giving her the odd Polo mint or treat, while any apples left in the rooms were fed to Sesky at the first opportunity. It was lovely to

Sesky on her 31ˢᵗ birthday, 2017.

see her out in the paddock enjoying herself while we had lunch and got on with our day. I suppose it's no wonder the bins outside the stable block took longer to empty when I was doing them.

For the first time in many years I was doing a completely new job, so different from what I had done most of my life, but I felt as though I had been in house-keeping forever. The good finishing times gave me plenty of riding time with Sesky, and she enjoyed all the attention from my fellow workers, especially on her birthday. I also had more time for checking what was happening with Shaki and the cows in my free time.

The following spring and summer brought some unusually hot weather, which made housekeeping a night-mare. The rooms were so warm without any heating on, and the doors and windows open, and I found it particu-larly hard to cope with as I'd worked outside for so many years. I missed the stable and teaching outdoors in the dry weather.

Finishing times could not come quickly enough, and I'd rush to get changed and take Sesky out for that much needed long ride. A breath of fresh air was the ending to many a hot day, before spending many long nights at the hospital for the past months with my mum, who was ill.

Sesky enjoyed her days in the paddocks, relaxing in the sun and being groomed for me when she came in, or having her bath on occasional days. She was always ready in no time, and we'd head off together to enjoy our special time. This always calmed me and gave me the strength to face the difficult trip to the hospital again.

When Mum sadly passed away that autumn, after a long illness, Sesky was my rock. I do not know how I would have pulled myself through without having her to take my mind off things. She was always there to make me smile, and I was also thankful for being in the housekeeping team.

The following year (2018), from February onwards, we had a tremendous amount of snow which caught many people out and made travelling almost impossible. A lot of our staff had to stay at work in the accommodation, as they were unable to get back out for days. I didn't mind, as I was beside my horse! The warm rooms were the most pleasant place to be working at that time, as walking outside was nearly impossible, and I was glad not to be working on the yard in those conditions.

Having Sesky in the Gold barn was perfect, as it meant I only needed to walk her a short distance inside to the school to ride. Even there, though, some snow had somehow managed to get through the high roof to land inside, and Sesky would jog round, snorting at the snow on the ground. I certainly appreciated the indoor school even more at this time, as it meant we hardly missed a day's riding throughout the winter months.

Sesky and me in 2018.

The birth of calves throughout the year, followed by the addition of little lambs, filled the sheds at Shaki's and finally made it feel like springtime was almost upon us. Sesky enjoyed her 32nd birthday and, bright as ever, added to the enjoyment as we started to get back outside again for our rides. With the paddocks opening back up, I loved seeing her enjoy her run for freedom and rolls in the grass. When the long days of light eventually arrived, we could ride out round the countryside roads and enjoy some of the lovely dry days and our peaceful time together. On the light drizzly days, we plumped for a short walk around about, after being in the school.

I was certainly not prepared for what happened in May that year. As always, I started my day by going into see

Sesky early before work. I'd ridden her the night before, and she had seemed her usual bright and cheeky self when I'd left her late that evening. But by morning, something had changed. There was not even a neigh when I slid the door open to go into the barn, which was really unlike Sesky. She always neighed loudly on seeing or hearing me.

That morning, she stood to the back of the stable and had hardly touched any of her haylage from the night before. When I put her feed in, she showed no interest in it apart from the odd mouthful, which concerned me. She did not have colic and there were no signs to show anything else, but she was definitely not right.

The girls on the yard kept me informed that morning, as I had to work, but when there was no change by lunchtime, I called the vet.

When I met him at Sesky's stable, he checked her over but was unable to give me an answer about what was wrong, so he took bloods to be sent away and checked. Throughout the day, she ate slight amounts of food and some haylage, but nowhere near normal.

Over the next few days, she went for a small in-hand walk with me into the school from time to time, and she improved after having some jags later. The vet thought she might have a virus, even though nothing was showing up in the bloods. She started slowly eating a little more and perked up for a few days, looking interested in what was going on again.

Sensing she was a bit better, I rode her about the school which she preferred, but only a bit in walk to cheer her up. I didn't do too much with her, as I could feel something was not right. The spark had gone from her, and nobody could work out why.

Over the next week or two, Sesky had more bloods taken, and more jags given. Following the injections, she always seemed to perk up slightly, but after a day or two was back down again. She was still only slightly eating feeds, haylage, and the warm bran mash I hand-fed to her at night.

Nothing seemed to work, and with the vets still not coming up with an answer and Sesky not improving, the situation was worrying.

I made the decision to move her to a quieter yard that I knew, where she would have just a few horses and ponies for company. The vet jagged Sesky to make her comfortable for the journey, then Iona and I moved her to her new home. That night, she settled down without any bother, which again was unusual, and that week there was still no change, and she showed no interest in her new surroundings.

I tried to walk her to a nearby paddock, with help, to encourage her to be out in the air with the sun and the fresh grass, but it made no difference, and it was difficult to get her walking. Her rugs were left on, as she had lost a fair bit of weight, and I would just stand helplessly beside her when she would not move from the spot.

By that time, I had left my job, as I did not want to carry on working there and wanted to spend all the time with Sesky, willing her to get better.

Sadly, the summer we had looked forward to was never to be. Within a few weeks of moving her, I had to face the heart-wrenching decision – after discussion with the vet – to let her go. After all sorts of tests and treatment, they had decided that some sort of cancer, which we hadn't known she had, was to blame for making her deteriorate so quickly. It had all been a terrible shock, as Sesky had never been ill.

When the horrible day came, I told myself to think of it as her going for a heavenly sleep. But it was my worst nightmare, and many times I wished I could wake up and everything would be fine!

Those 28 amazing years of having such a wonderful horse as Sesky seemed to have passed in the blink of an eye, and I am convinced she made me who am I today.

Three years on now, when I think of her, she still makes me smile. I guess in a way we were quite alike – determined, sometimes stubborn, but strong and determined to carry on. And just as Sesky, at 32 years young had always thought and acted like that cheeky, lively four-year-old that I first met, I guess I still think of myself as being the young person I was then, too!

As the place I had worked held too many memories of Sesky, I never went back. I thought it was time to find another job and move on, and being divorced that year brought to an end another chapter. Looking back over those last two years, I could never have imagined how things would turn out – from Mum passing away, to losing Sesky. These would have been the last two events I would have expected.

Through time, I soon found another housekeeping job which I enjoyed, and a while later my good friend Agnes joined me. We still work together after all these years, and on many a day as we work and chat about putting the world to rights, Sesky and all her mischievous times come into the conversation.

After a while, I decided to go back to freelance teaching, which got me back involved with horses again. And although it would never be the same without Sesky, Iona encouraged me to get back into the saddle again with her horses.

Many a night Shaki still has to put up with me trying to tell him about Sesky, chattering on while he just wants peace after a hard day of work. The expression on his face makes me laugh!

Nowadays, though, you will find me studying my lambing manual from the other year, while Shaki says all I need to know is 'two legs, head, and pull...'! I prefer to know more, reading and preparing for the lambing season ahead, refreshing the mind. Then, when we are constantly lambing at night, I get so excited that I can't help running to wake him and tell him when more are coming, while he shakes his head and puts his boots back on again. His jacket is then thrown on once again, as I run out of the door in front of him.

Baby lambs born on the farm.

Having taken up walking over the past few years, I love to wander around Loch Lomond and the surrounding area. It's my favourite place to be, and I thoroughly enjoy the views and peaceful days. Some of my favourite times are when I drive further out into the beautiful countryside, and to the little gem that is 'The Oak Tree Inn' at Balmaha. (That favourite oak tree name of mine!) A family-run business, it sits on the bonnie banks of the loch, beside the huge oak tree which is hundreds of years old. Its peaceful and tranquil setting is an ideal place to stay, or just to enjoy good food and friendly people, and where the staff make you feel most welcome. A home-ground coffee and ice cream is never to be missed from the coffee shop.

It's the perfect place to walk in the open countryside and forest tracks, along the water's edge, or to join the famous West Highland Way walk. And were I always wish I had Sesky to ride around on, to canter through the countryside, with her sparkling in the sunshine!

Often, I go back over some of the routes and fields where Sesky and I once used to ride, but now I cover the miles on foot, clocking up my daily step count which I add to a workout in the gym, focusing on beating whatever challenge I set.

I still reminisce about our rides together and think of the dreams I realised with her, and the ones I still hope to achieve. Including eventually going to Sesky's homeland in Ireland to visit the town named Seskinore, to ride a horse along one of the beautiful beaches there, and to dream that it is Sesky… just for that time…